THE FAIL-SAFE
SOLOPRENEUR

THE FAIL-SAFE SOLOPRENEUR

6 Essential Practices to Manage Your Well-Being Working for Yourself

DARREN C. JOE

Published by ASE

ISBN 978-1-7370231-1-1

Ebook ISBN 978-1-7370231-2-8

Visit the author's website at www.upstartist.tv

To the struggling entrepreneur - you are not alone.

Contents

INTRODUCTION
Always Two Sides   **1**

PRACTICE 1
What's Your Shadow?   **11**
Owning Your Dark Side

PRACTICE 2
Stuck? Seek Outsight   **26**
Evolving through Play & Experimentation

PRACTICE 3
Can You Manage Yourself Better than a Boss?   **46**
Dealing with Anxiety, Stress & Performance

PRACTICE 4
To Have or To Be?   **67**
Dealing with Instability & Failure

PRACTICE 5
What's Your Perfect Day?   **89**
Finding Meaning on the Pathless Path

PRACTICE 6
Who are You Grooming?   **110**
Dunbar & Dealing with Loneliness

CONCLUSION
Living The Questions   **130**

Acknowledgments   *137*
About the Author   *139*
Notes   *141*

"I decided to give my thoughts a form, to put them into practice, and so to determine whether my understanding was right or wrong."

- Masanobu Fukuoka

"What is and what is not create each other."

- Lao Tzu

INTRODUCTION

Always Two Sides

"If we were like other Chinese families, we would have disowned you already."

My mother's words cut through me. The woman who sacrificed her career to raise me, whose approval I craved more than anyone's, imploring me to move back home to California and start a "real" career. Time was running out.

"You're no spring chicken anymore, Darren. Get a job! Start a family. I'm so worried about you."

I had just turned 40 in Ho Chi Minh. I lived comfortably working two days a week and helped thousands of people get into the world's top business schools. I walked minutes to my daily essentials: work space, coffee, groceries, the park. I danced salsa three nights a week, watched matinees on Mondays, and spent weeks exploring Vietnam. I could do 60 pull-ups and had a six pack. And I spent every morning doing what I loved: writing and hosting a show.

But for the past 10 years, my Mom saw me as a failure. My dad, too, although he was more diplomatic about it. He referred to my work as "your entrepreneurial stuff," as if I should make my business what it really was: a side hustle.

I mean, I guess they did have a point.

My business was on track to make $30,000 USD. Less than I made during my first job 20 years ago, and less than half the average starting salary of my university's undergraduates. I had three part-time employees, but nothing else to show in terms of size. I was single and living alone. From their point of view, I needed to build capital, and roots, now.

Who was right?

Of course, I wanted to make more money. But I had complete control of my schedule. And I was doing what I'd do if I had all the money in the world: writing, hosting, teaching, dancing and traveling. Most days, I felt so lucky to live my life.

But other times, like during this conversation with Mom, I felt like a total failure. I hadn't had a job in 10 years, and my business had dipped. I had $100,000 in savings, but family and retirement required much more. During my prime earning years, I was making peanuts.

I'd had this tension ever since charting my own path. I had optimized my life for freedom. But by society's standards, I was a failure. "Wasting my education" as my Mom put it.

For the first 30 years of my life, I had succeeded on the conventional path. Valedictorian. Princeton University graduate. Analyst for leading companies. But the past 10 years were full of gray. There was no clear destination, no final exam to pass. How would I know if I made it? A fully funded retirement? Choosing who I worked with and what I worked on? Checking items off my bucket list? Was I on the right path... or any path at all?

I had to define my own rules for success.

More people are choosing to work independently, whether as independent contractors, as a side hustle, or as business owners. In 2019, 57 million Americans freelanced, comprising 35% of the US workforce, and the share of full-time freelancers increased from 17% in 2014 to 28% in 2019. Like me, most full-time freelancers choose this path so they can be their own boss, working when and where they want.

I've tasted that delicious freedom. My childhood dream was to live in South America. In 2015, I spent a year in Medellin, Colombia, dancing salsa every night. For the past 10 years, I vacation whenever I want - usually in the middle of the week to avoid the crowds. I've lived in the US, Vietnam and Taiwan and traveled to a dozen countries. I used to hate being stuck in an office as day turned to night. Now I'm outside exercising as the sun sets.

I am so grateful for a decade full of creative freedom, adventure, and meaning.

What I didn't expect was the cost: failure (F), anxiety (A), instability (I) and loneliness (L).

I call them the Four Horsemen of the self-employed life.

Accept that they will rear their ugly heads and paralyze you.

WORK-LIFE VALUE - COST

Let me quickly explain the sunny and shady sides of each mountain. By ingenuity, I mean being inventive and making something new. This is what entrepreneurs and creators love to do. Thomas Edison, whose inventions include the movie camera, phonograph and storage battery, famously failed thousands of times before inventing the lightbulb. The flip side of ingenuity is failure.

We all desire a work-life full of freedom. But with great freedom comes great responsibility. As we will explore later, having too much choice can paralyze. And instead of being happy about our choices, we often fret about the choices we didn't pick.

No instability, no adventure. They are two sides of the same coin. We love TV shows, sports and games precisely because we don't know the outcome. We admire history's great explorers for braving the unknown to make their discoveries.

Finally, in our quest for meaning - to make our dent in the world - we can feel isolated from loved ones, friends and a society who don't share the same vision. It can feel like no one cares as much or has as much to lose, and that you carry the entire burden of making something happen. Defining and living out your rules for success can also alienate you from society.

Failure, anxiety, instability, and loneliness (FAIL) are the price we must pay for charting our own path. The Taoist concept of yin-yang describes this the best: everything contains the seed of its opposite. FAIL is the shadow side of the mountain, the dark side of what we desire most as solopreneurs.

The cost of my glorious freedom? I spent a year in Colombia launching a forum for my customers. It totally failed. I spent weeks traveling across Vietnam, seeking inspiration; despite my business making the most money ever, I had never felt so lost. And all those late afternoons sweating in the park? That was to self-medicate against the devastation of Covid-19 on my business - I had lost a third of my customers.

Few mention this dark side of working independently. It's swept under the rug.

Some questions I've had over the past 10 years include:

- *I'm supporting myself, but this business feels like I'm always pushing a boulder uphill. Should I stick with it or try something else?*
- *Your peers make hundreds of thousands of dollars. What's wrong with you? Why are you such a failure?*
- *Would anyone care if I died tonight in this bed so far from home?*

How will the growing millions of solopreneurs manage the failure, anxiety, instability, and loneliness of this pathless path?

I believe three factors combine to make the self-employed life hard on our well-being.

First, entrepreneurship is brutal on our mental health. Entrepreneurs are twice as likely to suffer from depression as the general population, twice as likely to have suicidal thoughts, and three times more likely to suffer from substance abuse. Starting a business is stressful.

Second, working alone runs counter to 200,000 years of evolution. We evolved as social animals to connect and work in tribes. Today's technology and money system allow us to survive outside a group for the first time in human history. In 2018, the US had 26.5 million non-employer firms - those with no employees except the owners - a 70% increase from 20 years ago. And the share of adults who live alone has nearly doubled over the last 50 years.

According to the World Health Organization, people in wealthier countries suffer depression eight times as much as they do in poorer countries who rely much more on help from their community. Could one factor be that greater financial independence leads to more isolation, which results in higher rates of depression and suicide in affluent countries? Independent work is the tip of this iceberg, the ultimate expression of surviving outside a group.

Third, our education system does not prepare us to deal with ambiguity. In the classroom, we take multiple choice tests and operate in a black-and-white world of right and wrong. And most career planning still assumes an outdated industrial model with defined career paths and ladders to climb. The Institute for the Future forecasts that 85% of the jobs that will exist in 2030 haven't been invented yet, and McKinsey estimates 40% of US jobs are in occupations that are likely to shrink by 2030.

So, independent workers fight wars on three fronts: creating a sustainable business (which statistics show is highly unlikely), working outside a tribe (which runs against our evolutionary heritage), and designing careers in the face of extreme uncertainty (for which we are ill-equipped).

Is this freedom still worth it? Is there a way forward where independent workers can enjoy flexible work-lives and maintain their well-being?

Before each season, the National Basketball Association (NBA) runs a mandatory four-day "NBA Rookie Transition Program" to prepare rookies for their new lives. Current and former NBA players share their experiences dealing with life and challenges *outside basketball.* Financial experts advise how to avoid common financial pitfalls. Surviving the NBA is not easy. Sixty percent of NBA players go broke within five years of retirement, despite making tens or even hundreds of millions of dollars. Imagine being 19, one year removed from high school, and then becoming millionaire famous. How can players take care of loved ones and enjoy their new lifestyle without getting into debt? The workshop advises rookies on best practices to stay in the league and set themselves up for the future.

Similarly, this is a book about dealing with life and challenges *outside your business*, namely the Four Horsemen of failure, anxiety, instability, and loneliness. Consider this your solopreneur survival guide. There are plenty of books about how to make money. But just as important is managing your well-being outside your business, so you can stay in the game and make the most of your flexible work-life to live more and be more.

Engineers design machinery to be fail-safe, so that tools revert to a safe condition in the event of a breakdown or malfunction. Similarly, we solopreneurs need to design our working lives to be FAIL-safe, so that when failure (F), anxiety (A), instability (I) and loneliness (L) strike, we can re-center ourselves, learn from the experience, and do our best work again. FAIL-safe practices help us survive and enjoy our journey.

Over the next six chapters, I share stories from 10 years of making a living virtually and independently. I consider this survival an accomplishment. I hope they give you a taste of what's possible when working for yourself, and a clear view of the challenges. The journey never ends, but I describe how I and others have dealt with the inevitable failure, anxiety, instability, and loneliness of self-employment.

Each chapter is centered around one question I've found critical to survive and contains 4-5 exercises to help you design your FAIL-safe work-life. I encourage you to complete the prompts that resonate with you and let the rest soak in. At the end of the book, you can find the full list of tools to combat the Four Horsemen, which will be handy at different points in your journey.

Few talk about the most challenging aspect of working for yourself. It's not making money. It's managing your well-being. My experience has taught me that surviving the emotional rollercoaster - dealing with the Four Horsemen - is the key to thriving as an independent worker. This will be the biggest challenge for millions of people working for themselves: managing meaning and well-being.

What's Your Shadow?
Owning Your Dark Side

I lift my left foot up slowly and hold it in the air, keeping my balance and perfect toe point. And now, for the finale. I step into the corner and take a deep breath. I've practiced this final tumble hundreds of times, burning it into my muscle memory. I run across the blue floor and do a roundoff, back handspring, and back flip. I stick the landing perfectly.

Arms up triumphant, I turn to the judges and bow.

My coach hugs me. I walk over to the judge, scoring me out of 10 points. I hover over him like a schoolmaster. He flips two rings of numbers. First 9. And then 5. I hold the scorecard up to the audience. 9.5!

The camera pans up and away from me to the second floor, where my grandparents are watching. They turn towards the cameraman, my father, and chuckle. My grandpa gives a thumbs up.

The grainy video cuts to the awards ceremony. Dozens of kids sit in their leotards, fidgeting. They are awarding first, second, and third place, the overall champions for each age group. I'm 6 years old but competing in the 8-year old division. Third place is announced, then second place. The tension builds.

"And in first place, with an overall score of 9.4, Darren Joe!"

I walk to the front of the stage, and then onto the highest level of the podium. I bow as the organizer drapes my neck with a gold medal. I stand there chin down, self-conscious. But inside, I'm beaming. I was number one!

I know Mom and Dad will be proud.

I spent my childhood being the best.

- The #1 gymnast in Southern California
- The #1 tennis player in Ventura County
- The *Los Angeles Times* High School Athlete of the Year
- High School Valedictorian
- Graduating from Princeton University, ranked #1 in the US

But when I reflect on my childhood and what drove me to achieve, I think back to those grainy gymnastics videos.

I see myself executing rings, parallel bars and pommel horse routines flawlessly as a 6-year old.

I am embarrassed by how I intrude into the judges' personal space. *You better give me a good score.* I can feel the tension, the pressure to score high.

Being the best is what lit my parents' faces up. I can still see the looks on their faces now, chins slightly down, blushing half-smiles that screamed joy, pride and love all at once.

Decades later, I'm talking to my Dad. We're reminiscing about our weekends crisscrossing Southern California for junior tennis tournaments. I remember our warm-ups more than the matches, me rolling my eyes as another of my Dad's backhands sails long. *What awful warm-up is this?* Then reclining in the passenger seat as my Dad sped through Los Angeles traffic to get to the tournament site on time.

"Dad, I can't thank you enough for sacrificing your weekends for those tournaments. I'm sorry I was such a pain sometimes. But I'll always cherish those weekends together."

"Thanks, son. I'm glad we did that. But if you didn't end up getting into a good college, I'm not sure if it was worth it."

Wait, what?

I ask him to clarify.

"All that money and time we spent on tennis, it was worth it because you got into Princeton."

The end result justified the sacrifice. The silent ethos underpinning our relationship.

For 30 years, I thought I had the world's best parents: infinitely patient, supportive and loving. Unlike many of my friends, I had no childhood horror stories.

Only when I started my business did I realize my parents could be condescending and deaf to my dreams.

Now that I wasn't making good money or working for a prestigious company, I had lost their support - my bedrock. It was if someone had shattered the one thing I thought I could count on in life.

Since quitting my last job 10 years ago, every conversation with them would turn into a lecture about how I needed to fix my life that had fallen off the tracks. Like a broken record, I kept trying to win their approval with sales ("I got 3 new customers!"), prestige ("Look who I'm working with!"), or by using my flexible schedule to vacation with them ("Let's go to Zion National Park!"). But I could never seem to please them like before. I felt guilty for not being enough.

The script of *please mom and dad with results* running on an infinite loop, still driving so much of my happiness as a grown man.

Mom: "Darren, what happened to you? You've worked on your business for how many years now? You're barely making any money. To raise a son with so much potential, who gets a good education, and then he wastes it."

No 9.5 score to flash to the audience. No podium to climb. No gold medal. All their efforts. Just not worth it.

This childhood pattern of performing to earn love carried over into my relationships, too.

If I didn't have a girlfriend, it was because there was something wrong with me. If only I made more money, dressed better, or oozed more charisma, then I'd get a girl.

I felt pressure to perform on dates. Make my apartment sparkling clean. Go to a hip restaurant. Listen like a priest in confession. It was exhausting.

When I was 35, I met a woman in salsa class. She was gorgeous. She was one of the most loving human beings I'd ever met. She wanted to spend all her time with me.

I remember thinking, *Why does she love me? I don't have much money. I'm not the best looking guy. I can barely dance. Why do I deserve this beautiful woman's love?*

I tear up thinking about this, how I had gone through my entire adulthood thinking I had to perform to even qualify to be in a relationship. This belief was so ingrained that I thought it was normal.

And here was a woman in love with me for just being me. I didn't have to do anything.

How did you win love and acceptance growing up? What parts of yourself do you present to the world - and hide - to look like a success?

Winning gold medals won my parents' and society's admiration. So I kept doing so. My interests were secondary. I gravitated to music, dance, and writing in my free time. But external validation mattered more. Straight As and a top tennis ranking were the formula that would get me into elite universities.

This pleaser personality made me outwork and outperform my peers. It made me sensitive and empathetic to others' needs. It helped me quickly make friends and build trust with others.

But pleasing also held me back. I silenced my preferences to make others happy. I shied away from necessary conflict, hiding my true feelings. Worst of all, I felt a constant need to live up to expectations which were not my own.

Carl Jung, the famous Swiss psychoanalyst, wrote about how each of us has a shadow side - the part of us that we try to hide, that horrifies and disgusts us, that is prone to projection. While this shadow side often makes us stronger, driven or more creative, it also has the power to derail us.

"Everyone carries a shadow," Jung wrote, "Until you make the unconscious conscious, it will direct your life and you will call it fate."

Why did I find Mom's lectures so tiring? Why could I not stand Dad blaming others for his life mistakes? Why did I judge my friends on social media? Maybe because *I so often stubbornly did things my way.* Maybe because *I hated being so indecisive in my own life,* letting others dictate my choices. Maybe, just maybe, because *I felt phony,* presenting an adventurous persona publicly while struggling privately with my lack of courage.

I would bury these strong feelings of anger, frustration and judgement. By doing so, my shadow side remained hidden, the self-defeating story on repeat and the root of the problem unaddressed: *Darren, what's wrong with you? Mom and Dad have sacrificed so much to give you so many opportunities. Why are you so far behind in adulthood - achieving financial security, buying property, and starting a family? Once you do this, Mom and Dad will be on your side again. Then all will be okay.*

Despite pursuing my dream work-life full of autonomy, creativity and impact, I still drifted back to this invisible script from childhood, running for decades on autopilot. I would always be a failure unless I pleased my parents. I stood conflicted on the precipice of the work-life I desired.

I always felt torn in two directions, forging ahead to pursue my dreams while looking back for my parents' assurance.

We must turn and face our shadows. We can't get rid of them. But we can shine light on the deeply ingrained patterns of our childhood to maximize their advantages and manage their liabilities. Only when we embrace the hidden and non-acceptable aspects of ourselves can we evolve beyond our old, tired stories. Otherwise our shadows will continue to shape our behavior and businesses in unknown, often harmful ways.

The starting point for entrepreneurs is to see a reality that few others see and then marshal resources to serve that need. Getting to the truth of a situation, whether that be about a market, product or customer, is an important daily practice. And the most fundamental reality to see clearly is what drives you: the light and the dark.

This is about owning ALL parts of you - what's displayed outwardly and kept hidden from the world - so you can understand your default patterns of behavior that affect your work, relationships and business.

Three practices have helped me understand, accept and benefit from my shadow side.

Love Yourself When You Feel Scared, Angry & Ashamed

Yes, celebrate your success:
- Love yourself when you accomplish a goal
- Love yourself when you land a customer
- Love yourself when you travel to and work in a new city

But also welcome your unwanted feelings:
- Love yourself when you feel like a failure
- Love yourself when you feel pissed at a customer
- Love yourself when you feel lost as you choose your own adventure

Love means co-existing with and giving something space. Too often, we bury our negative feelings. This resistance keeps life complicated. We need to love the parts of ourselves that we feel are unloveable. It's okay to not be okay. All our emotions are valid. Only when we give these negative emotions and feelings space can we begin to see their origins.

I've learned that the shadow leaves clues in the form of intense feelings. Each time you feel angry, scared or resentful, there is a powerful lesson to be learned. The faults you righteously judge in others often mask what you feel about yourself. Don't push away emotions - especially the ones you feel should be forbidden.

This could be as simple as saying, *I love myself when I feel*

_____.

For example, *I love myself when I feel angry at Mom.*

Acknowledge your dark emotions and let them be. *I see you. You belong to me.* Don't ignore or run from them. Why might you be feeling this way?

> *It's okay to feel angry at Mom for not accepting your career choices. You feel so strongly because you love her, crave her approval and want her to be happy. But you can't blame her. She raised you and worked hard to live a stable life - she just wants the same for you. Don't take what she says so personally. She just wants the best for you.*

The first step is to reclaim the disowned parts of yourself. Shine light on the secrets and censored feelings that keep you stuck. Jung said it best: "I'd rather be whole than good."

How Are You the Master of Your Disaster?

In my case, I was setting myself up for failure with unrealistic expectations.

How could I expect my parents - career government workers who have lived in Los Angeles their entire adulthood - to approve of or even understand a location-independent entrepreneurial career?

By definition, adventure brings instability. Yet I pursued my adventure expecting the support of my parents, who above all else, crave stability in their lives and mine.

That's not only naive, but also a recipe for misery.

Letting go of that expectation frees up so much energy to succeed on my path.

Do I really want to keep spending my life trying to win my parents' approval - something outside my control no matter how brag-worthy my savings account, job or family?

Face your shadow. We all crave love, security and belonging. What's your pattern for getting them? Your childhood patterns of relating and being aren't necessarily positive. How are you responsible for creating the conditions of your suffering? Do your default stories still serve you?

The irony of our shadow is that most of our friends can see what holds us back, but they don't tell us because they don't want to hurt our feelings. Entrepreneur Jeff Booth calls this "The sign on our forehead."

Think about those closest to you. It's often blindingly obvious what's keeping them stuck. Many have an ego they're trying to protect that's telling them a different story. You don't want to hurt their feelings or risk conflict by exposing their blind spots. But what you're really saying is that you care more about what they think of you than them. If you have no problem discussing that person's flaws with others, why don't you share with the person directly?

What if we cultivated relationships of radical honesty? Our egos are brittle, but if we set the expectation to help each other see the unseen, we would take feedback not as criticism but as a generous sharing of perspective. I've told my best friends that if they think the woman I plan to marry is not the right fit, to tell me. Of course, I would make the final decision with my partner. But by setting expectations ahead of time, I won't take potentially negative feedback personally. I know they care so much about me that they have to tell me. I want their radical honesty. We should do the same for our professional lives.

The conversation could start like this: "I don't care if you change, but I have to tell you this because it's something I don't think you see." Delivered with love and care, that perspective could lead to major breakthroughs.

Own Your Entire Story

First, connect your past to your present. Who are you and where did you come from? How did that story shape your values and personality? Here is mine:

Growing up, I won my parents' affection through obedience and being the best, which made me a 'good boy.' Winning society's gold medals was the silent contract that determined the harmony of our relationship. I carried that pattern of relating into my career and relationships. I excel at listening, working hard and building trust. This script helped me succeed in school, sports and corporate life. It serves me less well as I chart my own path. I'm getting better at acknowledging and expressing what I truly want. I still depend on others' opinions - especially my parents' - for my self-worth. I am breaking the unhealthy habit of believing I need to be the best to earn love. I am flawed, and that's okay. All I can do is try my best. I am learning to cultivate my own voice and to be selective about whose feedback I value. I am the captain of my life, and I take full responsibility for my flaws, gifts, and choices.

What's your story?
This is where I come from. This is who I am.
Next, can you shine light on and accept all of you, including what makes you scared, ashamed and angry?

I'm scared that I'm falling behind in life and wasting my potential. I'm embarrassed about my income, especially for my age, and how small my life feels sometimes. Sometimes I resent the rich and powerful.

Finally, how can you respect and give healthy expression to your shadow feelings, qualities and experiences?

Status is at the core of your fears, insecurity and projections, no surprise, given your upbringing. Why not bring your competitive drive to being a world-class entrepreneur and communicator? See it as a game to be played - and mastered. Don't play the game to win Mom and Dad's approval, but rather your own satisfaction that you gave your best shot and competed with the best. Invest in people, education and environments so you can do your best work.

You're afraid of living small. You know you can be more. Instead of drawing inward and shrinking your domain, why not expand outward and embrace more people and resources to make things happen. Yes, life will be messier, and you'll have less independence. But you'll impact more people - and experience a richer life full of moments and memories.

It's taken me years to accept all parts of me and unravel my default loops. I'm still a work in progress. I wish I had done this shadow work earlier. It's empowering to write a new story, one that embraces all of you. This is the first step.

OWNING YOUR DARK SIDE

1. LOVE YOURSELF WHEN YOU FEEL...

PROUD
HAPPY
SUCCESSFUL

SCARED
ANGRY
ASHAMED

HERE TOO!

2. WHAT IS YOUR ORIGIN STORY?

THE GOOD

THE BAD

HOW CAN YOU RESPECT & GIVE HEALTHY
EXPRESSION TO ALL YOUR FEELINGS,
QUALITIES & EXPERIENCES?

Stuck? Seek Outsight
Evolving through Play & Experimentation

I quit my last job 10 years ago.

The day after, I woke up at 6:00am with an excitement that I hadn't felt in years. I finally had control over my day. I could do whatever I wanted! For years, I had struggled to get to work on time. Now I was up at the crack of dawn without an alarm.

The first six months were glorious. I devoured books and blogs and brainstormed business ideas on the backs of napkins. I attended friends' weddings and basked in my rebellious yet promising unemployment. The blank page and open road were intoxicating.

The next six months were spent building a website on Singapore MBA programs, my field of expertise, where I also provided admissions consulting services. Soon, I'd make a couple thousand dollars each month.

Soon never came. A year and half later, I hit rock bottom. I still hadn't landed a customer. A third of my savings had disappeared. What was I doing wrong? I had unrivaled expertise in the space. I had blogged consistently to grow traffic. And I had followed bestselling business books step-by-step. I was working harder than if I had a full-time job.

Maybe this whole thing was a big mistake. How would future employers view this long, unfruitful gap? Maybe I just wasn't meant to be an entrepreneur.

Each Thursday, I would tune into new episodes of the Tropical MBA Podcast, which featured location-independent entrepreneurs. The hosts were organizing their first conference in Bangkok, a short flight away.

None of my business ideas had gotten off the ground. I couldn't do this on my own. With my back against the wall, I bought a ticket to the conference. It would be my final attempt to make this life work.

The presentations were helpful. But more eye-opening was being with 40 location-independent entrepreneurs who were making a living selling cat furniture, condoms and yoga scheduling software - all online. They weren't any smarter than I was. They had just committed to this path – and stayed in the game long enough – to succeed.

I shared meals with Derek Sivers, who had sold his independent music business for $22 million dollars. Although the keynote speaker, he was as humble, grounded and eager to learn as newbies like me. It was a drastic change from the rigid hierarchies of the corporate world. Here was Derek, sitting next to me in a T-shirt and sandals, taking notes as a young 20-something talked about selling e-cigarettes in China. This world was not about age, status, or experience – it was about building what customers wanted.

A week after the conference, I made my first consulting sale. I had taken advice from a speaker to make my offer page frictionless and to reply to customers within a few hours. But just being with this group for three days changed my reference points for what was possible. I could do this!

One of the worst feelings as a solopreneur is feeling stuck. Speed and agility are your two greatest assets. So, losing momentum can feel devastating.

When this happened a year into my journey, I resorted to what had worked my entire life: studying harder. I tried to read my way into being an entrepreneur.

What I really needed were new reference points about what was possible: new relationships, new activities, and new ways of getting things done.

Customers don't care how hard you work. Yet here I was, stuck in worker-bee mode, believing that diligence would make me a business. What I really needed was more customer empathy and a better offer.

Professor Herminia Ibarra has researched workplace identity for decades. In her book *Act Like a Leader, Think Like a Leader*, she shares her research showing people become leaders by doing. She calls this outside-in approach to change outsight:

> "The outsight principle holds that the only way to think like a leader is to first act: to plunge yourself into new projects and activities, interact with very different kinds of people, and experiment with unfamiliar ways of getting things done. Those freshly challenging experiences and their outcomes will transform the habitual actions and thoughts that currently define your limits. In times of transition and uncertainty, thinking and introspection should follow action and experimentation—not vice versa."

It's hard to disagree with Professor Ibarra's logic:
- The way you think is a product of your past experience

- The only way to change how you think, therefore, is to do different things
- Doing new things – rather than thinking about new things – will accelerate your understanding of new roles and possibilities

I paid a non-refundable 18-months of life to learn this lesson: you can't think your way out of stuck.

The fastest way to transition to a new work identity is to meet people doing that work already, and to experiment with new activities and ways of getting things done. This is about adding new reference points and asking better questions.

I've studied how actors Heath Ledger and Joaquin Phoenix prepared to be the Joker. You can't think your way into becoming that diabolical. You have to imagine and play. Both actors kept a notebook to experiment with this new way of being. How does the Joker move? Laugh? Talk to others? Talk to himself?

It often helps to start with the physicality of a new role. The walk, slouch of the shoulders and curve of the back. Props like makeup, clothes and a gun can help spark experimentation too. Hence the power of masks over thousands of years. The mask gives you permission to become someone else entirely.

When you're stuck, how can you play and experiment more?

Imagine and Play with New Activities

- What would someone making $1,000,000/year focus on?
- What would a best-selling author's daily schedule be like?

Imagine and Play with New Ways of Being

- If you're used to being "baby brother," try being "big brother." If you're used to being the "star" and doing all the work, try being the "producer" and finding stars to do the work.
- If you were living your perfect day, how would you walk, talk and dress?

Imagine and Play with New Relationships

- Where can you find a group of people already doing what you want to do?
- If you had already achieved your goals as a business owner, who would you associate with?

My business, Touch MBA, came from a series of experiments. I loved podcasts and had been tuning into shows since the mid 2000s. Why not start a show where, as a former MBA Admissions Director, I share how applicants can get into their dream business schools?

I had never recorded a podcast. Nor did I consider myself a great public speaker. But I knew MBA applicants were tired of formal presentations that served as little more than marketing pitches. They wanted to know what schools were really like before making such a huge investment. And what better medium than podcasts to have in-depth conversations with Admissions Directors and MBA students about their business schools?

I still remember recording my first episode in 2012. I thought it was terrible. Why would anyone listen to this? But I reframed the podcast as play. What did I have to lose? I didn't have to tell anyone about it. I would just record episodes for a year and see if that grew traffic to my website.

It took me another week to learn how to edit and distribute the show. I took a deep breath and pressed publish. And then, every other week, I did so again, releasing 25 episodes the first year. I started to get a trickle of top caliber applicants, so I kept on going. Now, the *Touch MBA Podcast* is one of the top-ranked MBA podcasts on Apple Podcasts, and is our number one marketing channel for touchmba.com, where MBA applicants can get free business school guidance. Our business school partners pay us to advertise to our audience. And now most people know me as a podcaster, something I never even considered as a career.

The pivotal breakthroughs for the business also came from experimentation. Would business schools pay an annual subscription fee to reach our audience? Could we create a system that gave applicants customized admissions advice? Would successful applicants be interested in sharing their experience on our show, or even host the show? Our experiments didn't work most of the time. But a few did, and that's what has made all the difference.

Let me share one more example from salsa dancing. While practicing, my partners and I play with different scenarios. *Let's pretend we're performing in front of thousands of people. Let's pretend we're Cubans dancing in the 1920s. Let's dance this time with 200% flavor.* Experimenting and role-playing with different moods, situations and feelings leads to breakthroughs in movement and expression.

Kobe Bryant, one of the greatest basketball players of all-time, was revered for his unparalleled work-ethic and competitive drive. Yet when asked about how he pushes through limiting beliefs, he answered:

"The more we mature, the more responsible our dreams become, and the more governors we put on ourselves and our ability to dream and to reimagine... It's not a matter of pushing beyond your limitations or expectations, it's a matter of protecting your dreams and protecting your imagination...

that's really the key and when you do that the world just seems limitless."

Through play, I've discovered a wealth of potential, personality, and resourcefulness. We just need to use our atrophied muscle of imagination. Play helps us discover our total, full-set of capabilities. And it's a hell of a lot more fun than working hard.

The problem is that doing new things is scary. Transitions require us to move beyond our comfort zones and can trigger a strong countervailing impulse to protect our past identities. We easily retreat to old habits, especially those that have been rewarded in the past. As Ibarra writes: "The paradox of change is that the only way to alter the way we think is by doing the very things our habitual thinking keeps us from doing."

How can we make experimentation - doing something completely new - less threatening?

To me, this is the key question to get unstuck. If we can make experimentation easier and less threatening, we can accelerate the growth of our businesses and entrepreneurial know-how.

Below are four principles that help me stay outsight-oriented.

Make it Easy to Win

My friend Jimmy changed my life with a simple practice: doing a minimum number of pull-ups per day. It doesn't matter if that's 2, 10 or 100. Just work out every day and get a little better.

I started with 10 pull-ups. It sucked. My hands hurt, and I felt pathetic. But each day, I did at least 10. Soon, I upped that to 20/day, then 30/day. Now I'm at 60/day. Getting ripped is a nice side benefit too.

The best part? I look forward to my time with the bars. Hitting my daily pull-up quota is an easy win each day. And every day, I get a little stronger.

Over months, that momentum of daily discipline makes you feel unstoppable. It starts to feel so good, in fact, that you reach a point *where you feel worse for not practicing.*

Start small with your new activity. 10 pushups/day. 15 minutes of writing/day. Approaching 1 new customer/day. Practice every day and build up your capacity. This is about shortening the time to get positive reinforcement. Your motivation will be high because you know you can succeed - and while you're there, why not do a little more?

How can you design new tasks so that you know you can win? So that you look forward to the challenge of getting healthier, wealthier, and more productive?

Make it Safer to Play

"Thank you for organizing this challenge. I learned a ton."

It meant a lot to hear this from Matt. We had just finished our final call. The past month, we had committed to meet twice per week and test one business idea per week. It didn't matter if we asked for customer commitment through an email, website or Amazon listing, just that we asked.

We called it *The Dare to Suck Challenge*, based on legendary rock band Aerosmith's weekly "dare to suck" jam sessions (Aerosmith is the best-selling hard rock group of all time, having sold more than 150 million records).

Aerosmith singer Steven Tyler described how the band makes music: "Each one of us brings an idea that we think is probably terrible, and that we are embarrassed that we even have the idea. But we present it. And nine times out of ten, the idea is actually terrible. But one time out of ten you get 'Dude Looks Like a Lady.'"

Matt and I each dared to test four business ideas, no matter how terrible, and while none took off, we grew our skills, knowledge and courage to try.

Doing new activities is scary, especially when your business or reputation is on the line.

So, what if we made failure fun, social, and expected? *What if we dared to suck?*

My favorite way to do this is with what I call a master-mind challenge.

A mastermind is a small group of peers that gathers regularly to share problems, get guidance and keep each other accountable. Think of it like having a board of peer advisors. A challenge forces you to ship something by a certain deadline.

After 10 years consuming hundreds of books, podcasts and courses, I believe deliverable-based challenges – done with the right peers – are the best way to learn new skills, identify blind spots, and grow your business.

Solopreneurs face unique learning challenges. We're less concerned with certifications and the signal they provide to employers than developing our ability to add value quickly. Most of us work alone and with less resources, too. So, I believe working on real-life business projects with a group of practitioners is the best way to grow our skills - and stay motivated.

Books and podcasts are too often consumed passively.

Online courses have a completion rate of 10%.

Conferences inspire and connect but lack follow up.

And traditional degrees are too long or expensive.

Challenge masterminds combine the best of all formats. They force action – and real output – with peer account-ability. They provide a fun, safe space where we can dare to suck and learn faster – and from each other's mistakes, too.

And intimate, regular gatherings help us deepen relationships, build our networks, and gain new perspectives.

Today we can access lifetimes of knowledge with a few clicks. What's lacking is daring to suck, regular practice, and safe spaces to share, learn, and connect.

Choose Environments that Hold the Space for Your Desired Identity

I spent the first few months of unemployment in Singapore continuing the habits of my corporate life: $100 Saturday nights out and $30 Sunday brunches to recover. My friends were middle managers making six figures for multinational companies. As much as I loved my friends, I could no longer afford my previous lifestyle. I just couldn't justify those $30 avocado toasts - I needed every dollar to give my business a chance to get off the ground. Singapore was one of the most expensive cities in the world. And for good reason, too - its world-class infrastructure provided stability for the risk-averse.

I knew that if I stayed in Singapore I'd start thinking about jobs. Real or imagined, I felt the pressure to maintain a certain lifestyle and social status.

So, I packed up and moved to Ho Chi Minh. Vietnam had always been my favorite Southeast Asian country to visit: chaotic, untrodden, and full of youthful spirit and hustle. A rising Vietnamese middle class also fit well with an MBA-related business I wanted to start. And I could live at a similar standard for half of the cost.

Most of my friends were also trying to start their own businesses. Sunday brunches in Ho Chi Minh were held at someone's apartment, where the host could buy 20 fresh coconuts and 20 banh mi's for $30. Talks of last night's reverie were replaced by talks of marketing tools. I had found a city and community that supported my desired identity as an entrepreneur.

Sometimes we have to ditch familiar tribes for tribes that hold us in new space. This could be as drastic as moving to a new city (like I did) or as simple as finding other practitioners where you live. It also means leaning on friends and mentors who believe in your new, desired identity.

Do you think all professional athletes thought they were destined for superstardom from Day 1? Or was a parent or a coach, who kept believing, demanding and sacrificing, the "real MVP?" American Idol is so powerful because the show holds the space for dish washers to see themselves as rock stars. Ironically, it's often the believers who help the achievers realize their full potential.

This is counterintuitive, but speaks to the importance of environment in excelling in a new role. Few of us have the confidence and skills to switch working-identities so quickly.

So we must rig the game to get to that inflection point – where others see us in our new identity - faster.

For some, that could be putting themselves in boot-camp-like programs that force them to evolve. For others, it could be joining circles that live and breathe entrepreneurship.

Who do you know already living your perfect work day? How can you spend more time with them (hint: offer them something of value)? Where and when is the next gathering of people you want to be like? Go. Buy a ticket if you have to. It will change your life.

Make it Bigger than You

Heroes go beyond their limits for their family, friends, and country. Channel that same, greater power. I've interviewed over ten self-employed creatives on my podcast. A common theme of their career success was that pursuing a greater cause forced them to take action. I share three of their stories below.

As a child in Vietnam, Ho Thai Binh almost died twice - once from malaria and once from falling out of a second floor window. Growing up in fishing village, he listened to funeral music every night, as many fisherman drowned at sea. Since then, he has lived with a sense of urgency. "I've learned there doesn't need to be any good reason for you to die. I think, if those moments happened again, what would I regret? That drives me."

After graduating from one of Vietnam's top universities and then getting a Masters Degree in Australia, he returned to his hometown determined to make a difference. For five years, he worked for his city government, making $150 per month. The turning point came when his girlfriend told him, "What you're doing is nice, but there's no future." This got him thinking. Why couldn't someone achieve both financial benefit and make an impact?

In 2016, he met an Australian paramedic and Swiss-Vietnamese giving free first aid training in his hometown. There were no first aid training organizations in Vietnam, and the duo would fly to Vietnam six times a year to give free training sessions. Vietnam is notorious for its motorbike traffic. Ninety-five percent of traffic accident victims don't get first aid, and over 50% of cardiac arrest victims die before reaching the hospital because most don't get CPR.

Using his programming and marketing skills, Binh volunteered to help the founders create Vietnam's first mobile app for first aid and organize more first aid training programs. Within five years, Survival Skills Vietnam has provided free and paid first aid education to 35,000 people in Vietnam. Binh now runs the organization full-time. "This is the only life I have, so I want to make it meaningful."

As a 10 year old, Yous Sopanha lost his father and over 100 relatives when the Khmer Rouge took over Cambodia. Despite holding two degrees and working as a high school teacher, Sopanha moved to Siem Reap - famous for Angkor Wat - to become an independent tour guide to support his family.

> "In Cambodia, the husband must look after the wife's family, so I have a lot of responsibility. I have to provide for my wife's parents, my sister-in-law and her two children, six orphan girls whose father was killed in the war, and my only son. Twelve of us live together in a small house. We all sleep on the floor in the same room. Most men would run a mile from my situation, but I don't care. I love my family so much I would do anything for them. I have many health problems, but I have to be strong for my family… Even though I'm a simple man I have a lot of people I can help. What I can help and do, I do."

Boo Junfeng has written and directed two feature films – *Sandcastle* (2010), which was the first Singapore film to be invited to International Critics Week at the Cannes Film Festival, and *Apprentice* (2016), which was Singapore's entry for the best foreign-language film category at the Oscars. *Apprentice* tells the story of a prison officer who is apprenticed to carry out executions in Singapore, which has a zero-tolerance policy for illegal drugs (Singapore is one of only four countries to still execute people for drug-related offenses). Writing and filming *Apprentice* took 6 years due to funding and production delays, but Junfeng kept going because "the ideas were too important."

What matters so much to you that you have no choice but to go beyond your comfort zone?

Making it bigger than you is also about channeling greater forces through you.

Psychoanalysts Robert Moore and Doug Gillette discuss this in their landmark book *King, Warrior, Magician, Lover*. They counsel men to access these four masculine archetypal energies through conversation, invocation, study, and acting. As explained in Chapter 1, I've long struggled with stepping out of my parents' shadow. I've drawn tremendous outsight from invoking King energy and imagery to be more purposeful and decisive in ruling my "kingdom." *If I were a King, how would I approach this decision, problem or relationship?*

In intimidating situations, Oprah Winfrey does this by reciting a line from Maya Angelou's poem, "I come as one, but I stand as ten thousand" and summons the courage of the ancestors and women who came before her. "I step into the room, not just as myself, but I bring that energy with me."

Channeling greater forces through you - whether that be from God, your ancestors, or the deep recesses of your psyche - unleashes your imagination and courage to take action.

Speed and agility are our two greatest assets as solopreneurs. We must adapt quickly to new market structures, industries and opportunities. The way to maximize our advantage in the market is to pursue outsight - an action-orientation towards challenging experiences that expands our frame of reference and capabilities.

This forces us outside our familiar identities. And we can feel like frauds when we switch friends, activities and ways of being so quickly. We can make experimentation less scary by making it easier to win, creating safe spaces to fail, finding supportive environments and drawing on powers greater than ourselves.

Whenever I'm stagnant, I seek outsight. This runs against today's startup culture which worships hustle. New people, activities, and ways of being are what change our perspective about our business and ourselves. What's needed is more imagination, play and experimentation - not more hard work.

STUCK? SEEK OUTSIGHT

HOW CAN YOU EXPERIMENT WITH...	NEW PROJECTS / ACTIVITIES?		DIFFERENT PEOPLE?		UNFAMILIAR WAYS OF GETTING THINGS DONE?
	_____ _____ _____		_____ _____ _____		_____ _____ _____

THEN, HOW CAN YOU MAKE...	EASY TO WIN?	SAFE TO PLAY?	BIGGER THAN YOU?	SUPPORTED BY ENVIRONMENT?
	_____ _____ _____	_____ _____ _____	_____ _____ _____	_____ _____ _____

Can You Manage Yourself Better than a Boss?
Dealing with Anxiety, Stress & Performance

When I was 25, I was lucky to be recruited by a prominent businessman to work in New York City. He was Vice Chairman of the world's largest scientific publishing company, with 7,000 employees across the globe. I would be his analyst and help the company improve its reputation with academics, librarians, and government officials around the world.

I met with him on a Saturday morning, after arriving from a 20-hour flight from Beijing. After welcoming me to the Park Avenue headquarters, he handed me a brand new Blackberry. It was smooth and sleek, the nicest phone I'd ever had. "Please keep this with you."

Three months later, I'm working out at the gym. I had decided to leave my Blackberry at home. I needed a break.

Each incoming email would trigger a blinking red light. Most were from my boss. He was tireless, waking up at 5am to catch the morning train from New Jersey into Manhattan, and then leaving late at night, after leading a number of community engagements. His responsibilities, output, and response time were astounding. But for me, it was nerve-racking; I was one red blink away from grinding his machine to a halt. I finished a hour-long boxing class and then enjoyed a long, cool-down stretch. The workout - and mental space - was wonderful.

The next day, my boss summoned me into the office.

"Why didn't you respond to my message last night?"

Oh shit.

"I was at the gym."

A long pause. He stared at me, incredulity morphing into disgust.

"Darren, you know why I got you that Blackberry, right?"

I knew the answer but was too proud to answer.

"Don't do it again."

We all have awful boss stories. And most of us choose to work for ourselves so we never have to report to someone ever again. But the irony of self-employment is you need to manage yourself better than a boss. Your livelihood and well-being count on it.

It's a strange situation to be in. No one is watching you. You don't have to get to work by 8am or respond to anyone. You set the rules. Want to work in your underwear all day? Go ahead.

On the flip side, your business is all consuming. Fire here. Your website is down. Fire there. Your bank account is frozen. Fire! A customer needs a reply. And on and on. You can never escape it. And when you do, even for an afternoon or weekend, you feel guilty for leaving your baby behind. You can always do more.

That's the paradox of working solo. You need to use all your faculties to get work done and to stop working. Like holding two opposing ideas in your mind, it's difficult to honor both.

I've found that willpower can only take me so far. Just as companies need strong corporate governance to stay on target, I need reporting structures to keep me accountable. I must also institute checks and balances and rituals to keep me from self-destructing. And do all this without a boss, because I'm never going back.

Take Time Off Seriously

Hustle! Grind! Crush it!

Bullshit.

Asking entrepreneurs to work non-stop from morning to night until their business succeeds is horrible advice.

That's like asking a professional athlete for his or her peak performance, 8 hours a day, 6 days a week, for months on end. Humans are not machines.

Our energy waxes and wanes, and we need deadlines to signal rest and recovery. Because business never stops, I set finishing lines: 7pm on weekdays, 2pm on Saturdays, and absolutely no work on Sundays.

More than anything, this is to give myself permission to rest. *It's okay.*

I remind myself that I chose this life so I could watch a movie Monday afternoon or dance in the park Friday as the sun sets. Each week, I schedule play time before work time.

You need to refuel your tank, not just to survive, but to do your best work. For most of us, our careers are marathons. It's about staying in the game long enough to strike gold; we have to be skilled, present and prepared to catch the few big waves that will make all the difference.

Sure, sometimes you will need to sprint and push harder than normal. But those sprints should be matched with proportionate intervals of rest.

Limiting work time reminds me that work is precious, and that I only have so many good hours a day to make something people cherish. When time runs out, I look forward to tomorrow. The more limits I set on work, the more productive I am. Without limits that make it scarce, work becomes a chore, or worse, my default mode of being and complete identity.

I've learned to take vacations as seriously as my business, too. Vacation gives you a finish line to look forward to. Every quarter, I schedule in 1 full week of disconnected, guilt-free rest. I always come bouncing back with new ideas and a renewed sense of purpose. Purposeful disengagement is necessary to fuel full engagement at work.

Michael Gelb, author of *How to Think Like Leonardo da Vinci,* asked thousands of people when they get their best ideas, and most people responded "in the shower," "resting in bed," "walking in nature," or "listening to music" – leisurely activities. Almost no one replied, "at work."

Guilt-free time off is necessary for peak performance – and a richer life.

Problem-Focused Coping

Stress can be a good thing, but not when experienced over long periods of time. Unfortunately, chronic stress is common for founders; there are always pressing deadlines, decisions and emergencies when running a company.

Chronic stress is related to every chronic health problem: heart disease, obesity, diabetes, cancer, and more.

Dr. Sherry Walling, a licensed clinical psychologist and entrepreneur, suggests two ways to deal with stress: problem-focused coping and emotion-focused coping. I've found both methods helpful.

Problem-focused coping recognizes that stress exists and actively deals with it. The idea is to cut out as many stressors as possible. It's about changing your mindset: you can control how much stress you experience instead of being a defenseless victim.

List the stressors in your life. How can you can eliminate or decrease these experiences?

I find it crazy that we give hundreds - if not thousands - of people the power to interrupt us anytime through messaging apps. Not only can any of my contacts message me, but they also expect a prompt response. That's stressful! I have to stay on top of 7 chat apps and 3 different work emails. And we haven't even gotten to the drugs of Facebook, Instagram and YouTube that make mind-numbing bliss one click away. And I thought my Blackberry in the mid 2000s was bad. How can anyone manage this deluge of communication and distraction?

Yesterday, I had planned to spend the morning writing. After waking up, I mindlessly checked my phone. I had forgotten to book a hotel for an upcoming group vacation, so I hurried to get it done. The original hotel was sold out. My friends and I had to figure out another one, which took dozens of messages over 3 hours. Bye bye sweet morning of productivity. The whole episode could have waited until the evening. One message at the start of your morning can send you into a tailspin.

That's why I don't check chat apps or social media before 11am. I also designate Wednesday afternoons and Sundays as "digital shabbats," when I leave my phone at home and raise a middle finger to the giant tech companies monopolizing my attention.

I've gone on a number of digitally-restricted week-long vacations, and found (sadly? happily?) that I'm not that important. I might lose a customer or annoy a friend, but my business and life never fall apart. Even if I miss 239 messages, hardly any notifications matter. Life is one screen away. A hard "no app before 11am" policy helps me avoid a lot of unnecessary stress. I understand not everyone can do this. The point is to design rules that make your work day less stressful.

Another way we can problem solve stress is to re-design our work activities so that we achieve flow at the edge of our capabilities, instead of being disengaged or frazzled. Being in a flow state happens when you're completely absorbed in and energized by the task at hand. One way to find flow is to map out where your task lies on two axes:

difficulty level (low to high) and your skill level (low to high). Flow happens when your skill level matches the activity's difficulty level.

As a lead in salsa, it's important to dance close to your partner's level so the follow feels comfortable and can enjoy the music (this applies the other way as well). From that foundation, you can challenge each other, improvise, and make magic happen. Too easy and they're bored. Too difficult and they're frazzled. You can see it on their faces.

The next time you're struggling with work, feel your face. Is it tied in knots or dull and listless? How can you redesign your work projects so they are at just the right level of skill and difficulty? My method is to divide projects into 50-minute sprints, with an appropriately challenging amount of work. Equally important is finding environments conducive to these bursts of deep work, where you're not distracted or interrupted. I've learned that the right level of sound, temperature, and space can make the difference between a frustrating or productive day. We can listen to our level of stress the same way we listen to a dance partner, and then respond appropriately. Taking a step back and thinking about what environments and structures make us look forward to work is one way to decrease stress.

Emotion-Focused Coping

Emotion-focused coping doesn't attack the problem (the stressor), but instead the emotions that come with it. Not all stressors are problem-solvable, but you can counterbalance stress with calm.

I'll never forget reading Dr. James Loehr's *Mental Toughness Training for Sports* as an 11-year-old competitive junior tennis player. Dr. Loehr had worked with tennis world #1s Jim Courier and Monica Seles, among others. What I most remember is the importance of rituals between points - how to make the most of the time between points to recover physically, mentally and emotionally in order to compete at the highest level.

Winner or unforced error, what you needed were rituals to bring your attention back to the present moment. Moving your strings back in place. Taking a deep breath. Bouncing on your toes before returning serve. Reminding yourself of your game plan. Centering yourself with phrases about welcoming and loving the challenge! You couldn't control your opponent - or the result. But you could control your physiology to compete at your highest level.

Emotion-focused coping is the equivalent to those rituals between points. Solopreneurs are athletes, after all; to perform our best, we need physical practices and rituals that give us optimal energy and states of being.

We can counterbalance stress with calm by:

Reframing our stressors. For example, dealing with customers is not a burden but rather the best way to gain insights for future products. Deep resistance to certain types of work is not a burden but rather a cry for you to hire someone and evolve your role and skillset.

Practicing activities that calm our entire being like yoga, meditation and prayer. My natural medicines for calm are nature, silence, dancing, and exercising outside. I've learned that the most important time for calming activities is when I don't have time for them.

Designating real-life "happy places" where you go to refresh your body and mind. This could be a park, lake or mountain near your home, a coffee shop or spa, or even a corner of your apartment. Make sure you have a physical place your body associates with rest and calm. Allow yourself periodic breaks to go there and fully recharge.

Taking regular vacations. Research has shown that people who give their minds a break are better able to think creatively and to solve problems. Rest and recovery are necessary for our best performance.

Generosity is one of my cherished values. But for a large part of my independent working career, I forgot that generosity towards myself counts, too. Designing daily, weekly and quarterly rituals to recover between work projects has aided my well-being immensely. Giving myself permission to be relaxed, happy and free is half the battle to combat the chronic stress of business ownership. Idle time and an open mind often lead to your best ideas, too.

Guardrails

In the 1920s, Carl Jung theorized that much of people's behavior is due to basic differences in the way they perceive the world and come to conclusions about what they perceive.

Isabelle Briggs Myers and her mother, Katherine Briggs, developed the Myers-Briggs Type Indicator (MBTI) personality inventory in the 1940s to make Jung's theory more accessible, by identifying 16 personality types that result from these preferences:

- "Favorite world: Do you prefer to focus on the outer world or on your own inner world? This is called Extraversion (E) or Introversion (I).
- Information: Do you prefer to focus on the basic information you take in or do you prefer to interpret and add meaning? This is called Sensing (S) or Intuition (N).

- Decisions: When making decisions, do you prefer to first look at logic and consistency or first look at the people and special circumstances? This is called Thinking (T) or Feeling (F).
- Structure: In dealing with the outside world, do you prefer to get things decided or do you prefer to stay open to new information and options? This is called Judging (J) or Perceiving (P)."

I recommend taking the MBTI or if you have less time, the free test at 16personalities.com, to identify your preferences and learn your personality type's strengths and weaknesses. Your preferences and blind spots are two sides of the same coin.

As an ENFP personality type, I see ideas and possibility everywhere. Every scribble on the blank page could be a million dollar, life-changing idea. I believe in my friends' dreams more than they do. Even when it seems impossible or ridiculous, I take the first step.

Yet, too often, it is only one step. A month later, I've started two other projects but finished none. In creeps the doubt, followed by paralysis. Is this the best idea? Should I pursue another instead? The endless possibilities splinter my effort, leaving me right where I started.

Left unattended, our strengths can quickly become weaknesses.

In the same way guardrails prevent motorists from driving off the road, we need guardrails to do our best work and to keep our strengths strengths.

We need to step outside of ourselves and imagine helping ourselves as we would a good friend or rock-star employee. In what environment would this person thrive? Where, when and why does this person fall off the track? What guardrails would keep this person moving the right direction?

When I read about ENFPs in the book *Do What You Are*, it was as if the authors knew me better than I knew myself. Their quote to describe ENFPs, "Anything is possible," could have been my personal motto. The book accurately described my biggest weaknesses too: difficulty focusing, poor practical skills, and a tendency to start many projects but finish few. Bingo!

What ENFPs must do to succeed is prioritize and follow through.

Once you know your habitual blind spots, you know where to put guardrails. Below, you can see just how detailed I am about creating rules that harness my innate tendencies and protect against their liabilities. It's humbling to admit your flaws. But the sooner you accept them and design around them, the farther you can go. No one will do this for us. If you were responsible for helping yourself, what would you do?

....

Example: Darren's Guardrails

Blind Spot 1: Difficulty Focusing, Easily Distracted

Guardrail 1.1: Keep goals front and center

My goals are posted on my bedroom mirror. They are also conspicuous in my daily and weekly reviews. This might sound like overkill, but it is exactly what I need to fence in my impulsive nature.

Guardrail 1.2: Limit number of goals per time period

My rule is to never have more than three tasks, goals, or projects per time period. For example, never have more than three to do's each day, or three goals for the year. Ideally, there is only one goal per time period. What absolutely must get done this week, month, quarter, year?

Guardrail 1.3: Work in time blocks i.e. 25 and 50-minute sprints

Scheduling and working in time sprints has been my number one antidote to distraction. I commit to one piece of work – whether writing, podcasting, responding to emails – for a minimum of 25 minutes. No phone, no social media, nothing else! I've found 50 minutes ideal to enter a flow state without fatigue. Perhaps this is conditioned from my child-hood education that broke classes into 50-minute blocks. Your most important goals deserve a minimum number of time blocks/day.

Blind Spot 2: Difficulty Following Through, Poor Practical Skills

Guardrail 2.1: Find accountability partners

Joining an accountability group helped my business immeasurably. Once a week, I'd have to tell four other entrepreneurs whether I accomplished last week's goals. Group members also helped me think through my priorities. Outsiders can often see your situation more clearly.

Guardrail 2.2: Require deadlines and deliverables for ideas

Deadlines and deliverables force follow-through. ENFPs tend to overthink everything, which leaves many projects unfinished. Therefore, I seek out events with peer pressure that end with a deliverable. My favorite method is to organize a group challenge where we each need to make something by a certain date.

Guardrail 2.3: Hire people to do routine and repetitive work
I'm embarrassed to say that only in my late 20s did I realize some people love to do administrative work, which I despise. Hiring people forces me to build systems so value can be delivered without me.

Guardrail 2.4: Work with realistic, practical people
I surround myself with practical people to anchor my idealism. In my first business, we had three partners. Two of us obsessed over business models and company culture. Our third partner – a serial entrepreneur – pulled us aside one day to think like "Chinese business man" (said with a fully racist accent as only a Chinese himself could). What materials did we need to design our shop? How much cash did we need for the next three months? He kept our focus on what had to be done right now. We would have never launched the business without him.

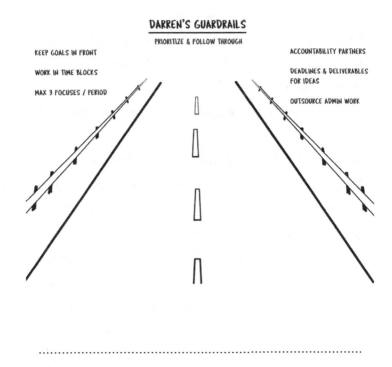

Who Keeps You Accountable?

I don't care if you're more disciplined than Sun Tzu or as self-aware as the Buddha. It's nearly impossible to manage yourself on your own. As social animals, we are built to seek status and meaning within a group. Getting outside perspectives is invaluable, and nothing keeps you more accountable than peer pressure.

After attending the conference in Bangkok, I realized the importance of surrounding myself with peers. We could learn from each other's experiences and raise each other up collectively. The best way to do this, I found, was to participate in a mastermind.

A mastermind is a group of practitioners (2-5 people) that meet regularly for accountability and to get outside perspectives. They're modeled after Benjamin Franklin's legendary Juntos in the eighteenth century, when a group of men from diverse backgrounds gathered in the spirit of mutual improvement.

Our group of business owners was led by Chris Kirkland, whose business allowed artists to showcase their portfolios online. Over months, we supported each other through product launches and tough business decisions. One member, Dan Norris, struggled to gain traction with his product - a web analytics dashboard. With two weeks of savings left, he launched WPCurve, which gave customers unlimited WordPress fixes for $59/month. That eventually became a million-dollar business, which he sold to GoDaddy. He has since gone on to write a number of best-selling books, including *The 7 Day Startup*, and start a microbrewery in Australia. During this mastermind, Chris also launched Tokyo Cheapo, which explored how tourists could experience the notoriously expensive city on a budget. The Cheapo brand has now expanded to include Hong Kong, London and Singapore as well.

What struck me was how Chris and Dan didn't need to work 100-hour weeks to get their businesses off the ground.

They just focused on a few key activities. Chris was living in Ho Chi Minh then, and I just remember him drinking a lot of coconuts. I'll also never forget when Dan, who had two kids, told us that he never works on weekends. He was easily the most prolific of our group. These real-life case studies multiplied my perspective and knowledge of what was possible.

There are many formats depending on the size and needs of the group, but I found weekly 1-hour meetings the most effective. We would spend the first 15 minutes sharing what we did last week and our goals for the next week. Then, one or two members would take the "hot seat" and solicit guidance on a pressing business problem. Until then, I had underestimated the power of psychological distance and diverse perspectives in seeing a situation clearly. Often times, we're too close to our work to see the bigger picture.

Since then, I have participated in several masterminds and organized a few of my own. I have found no better way to keep myself on track and build deep relationships with other entrepreneurs.

Be Like Your Best Boss

In my last job, I helped launch the flagship MBA program for Singapore's national university focused on business education. The program director, Doris, had assembled a small but effective team. I did the marketing and admissions. Norvin did career services. And Valarie managed the program logistics. It felt like a family. We worked well together, enjoyed each other's company, and rose to the challenge. We competed against business schools with bigger teams, budgets, and reputations. But within three years, we attracted world-class applicants, and soon after became a top-ranked program worldwide.

She was the best boss I ever had. Later, I found out that she had insulated our team from the politics that often plague universities. She had put us in the right roles so our strengths could shine. She was quick to sense what would derail team members and cleared those paths. Unlike my previous bosses, she gathered the group to celebrate holidays, birthdays and personal accomplishments. She left the office around 5pm every day and encouraged us to take time off. Work was challenging, but also a joy.

I think of Doris often when trying to recreate a high performance work environment. When I asked her for best management advice, she said, "Each person is different and should be managed differently."

We must see ourselves in the third person. Imagine that you are the boss responsible for creating the the ideal working environment for this person. What are his or her strengths and habitual blindspots? What structures, rituals and rules will keep him or her accountable, healthy and sane? Those accountability mechanisms and check and balance systems will be different for each of us. But install them we must - it's the only way I've found to manage myself better than a boss.

LESS ANXIETY	MORE PRODUCTIVITY
PROBLEM-BASED COPING	**GUARDRAILS**
LIST STRESSORS CAN YOU DECREASE OR ELIMINATE?	MANAGE YOUR BLIND SPOTS
EMOTION-BASED COPING	**WHO KEEPS YOU ACCOUNTABLE?**
TAKE TIME OFF SERIOUSLY PRACTICE ACTIVITIES THAT CALM DESIGNATE REAL LIFE HAPPY PLACES	MASTERMIND GROUP ACCOUNTABILITY PARTNERS EMPLOYEES

To Have or To Be?
Dealing with Instability & Failure

Why can't I sleep? Damn it.

It's 3am. I'm tossing and turning in bed. I'm trying to stop the waves of doubt rocking me from all directions. They are merciless. If I can just go to sleep, then maybe they will go away.

One of my long-time customers had canceled their contract. I don't know what else I could have done. We sent them exactly what they wanted - elite applicant leads, a number of whom ended up enrolling as students. They got massive return on their investment. I had serviced them the best I could, responding promptly to their requests for years. Their action shocked me.

It ruined my night. I suddenly felt lost, without ballast. I skipped dinner with my friends. I didn't want to see anyone. Just drift along and numb myself with empty chatter. Sports podcasts. Celebrity gossip. Talking heads, voices in the background. Crack a beer. Just lie there, comatose, avoiding the real issues for as long as possible.

They came roaring back late at night, as I lay in bed alone, staring at the ceiling.

Why did they cancel? I did everything for them and more.

What am I doing with this business?

What am I doing with my life?

Time is running out. What happened to you?

Why are you still pursuing this pipe dream?

Why are you such a failure?

One customer leaving triggering an avalanche of self-criticism. I feel defenseless to the piercing questions that don't stop. Sleep is the only way out of this echo chamber, and it's not coming any time soon.

Thank God that night wasn't the first time.

Over the years, I identified the pattern. The panic attacks always happen in bed. There is the late night version, where a thousand arrows of doubt rain on me from all directions. There's the late morning version, too. The sun is up high, but my curtains are drawn. I just lay there, avoiding the day, lethargic and dull. It's strangely soothing to stay in this cocoon state, while your business burns down.

At least in this muted stand-by mode, you can't feel much of anything: urgency, fires, failure.

Both usually come after a troubling realization about money. It could be a customer leaving or a profit and loss spreadsheet. This instability, the price we pay for pursuing our business adventures, is always lurking around the corner, ready to strike. Instability's best buddy is failure, and they like to gang up and attack you at the same time. They make a devastating combination.

It's no surprise that being able to put enough money into savings, saving for retirement and unpredictable income are the top three concerns for freelancers. Freelancers are more likely to feel they are living paycheck to paycheck than traditional employees. And most entrepreneurs need a couple tries or multiple pivots to find a sustainable business model. Failure and financial instability are part and parcel of being self-employed.

I've learned to ride out the panic attacks over money and failure. I let time - and a heightened vigilance to get good sleep, food, and exercise - work its wonders until I can see my situation more clearly. That doesn't make living with instability any easier. But at least I know there is light at the end of the tunnel; I've made it through before.

Making money is not the topic of this book. I know it can be all-consuming and even more stressful for those independent workers with families to support. I spent years launching products - most of which failed - before establishing my business. But I think we make this challenge even more difficult by equating our income with self-worth and making unhealthy comparisons, both unnecessary burdens. How can we shed this deadweight, so we can be lighter, adjust quicker, and move forward?

To Have or To Be?

I'm embarrassed to admit that for a long time I conflated income for self-worth. This only got worse when I started my business, because to society, money determines your worth as an entrepreneur. How [founder] made [large amount of money] in [short amount of time] is a guaranteed winning headline for small business media. "Doing well" in startup circles means making good money, not well-being.

It's not totally our fault. We swim in a capitalist culture that encourages us to equate what we have for what we are. We have a strong property orientation:

- not "I earn," but "I have money"
- not "I work," but "I have a job"
- not "I love," but "I have a wife"

But what happens if we lose our money, status, and relationships? If we are what we have, and we lose what we have, then who are we?

In a world where having is the dominant marker of status, is it surprising that millionaires with five million dollars don't feel wealthy and the top 1% of Americans hold 15 times more wealth than the bottom 50% combined? Having is a precariously relative existence. No wonder we struggle with greed and scarcity mindsets. This desire to have - and fear to lose - fuels our chronic sense of instability.

What if we identified with being instead of having? Then, I am no less a person if I have less money than you. I am no less a man if I don't have a partner. And I am no less an entrepreneur if my business is smaller than yours. Being makes living light and less stressful; it unloads the massive burden of having.

The beauty of a being-based identity is that being is inexhaustible. Unlike money, the more you spend, the more you have. Loving is easier the more you love. Giving is easier the more you give. Creating is easier the more you create. As Lao Tzu wrote, "The sage does not hoard. The more he does for others, the more he has. The more he thereby gives to others, the ever more he gets."

Being also leaves a much more powerful legacy than having. When I think about cherished people who have passed away, I remember them not for what they had, but for what they gave: their love, support, and example. All the having in the world means nothing if not shared.

I understand all too well that we need a base level of material possessions to survive. Existential having of food, shelter, clothes and medicine is necessary. But most of us have enough for our basic needs and are privileged to be among the billion people making more than $32/day, which qualifies us as the top 15% of the population. So why does having still dictate so much of our lives? I hate that this instinct to have - whether it's a partner, house or millions to retire - has driven so much of my life. I've lived decades with this forefront on my mind. Do I really want to spend the rest of my life measuring my life by having?

It's an unwinnable game - and even if you do eventually have a lot, your victory is short-lived as all of it can be taken away.

How can you shift your identity from having to being?

Instead of defining my entrepreneurial identity by money, I now define it by always creating value for employees, customers, and partners. That's what entrepreneurs do. I aspire to delight customers so much, they are happy to pay for my products and services. I do this whether I am making $5 or $5 million dollars. Doing this every day will eventually be rewarded by the market.

Examine Your Money Beliefs

We make our lives much harder by letting our money beliefs go unchecked. These beliefs hold us back.

Even though I was impacting thousands of lives, supporting myself, and spending the day doing work I loved, I couldn't stand that I was making less money than fresh college graduates. This irked me. My competitive nature couldn't let this go. Money is one of the world's few universal yardsticks, and here I was falling well short. I carried this insecurity with me, even when my business supported my dreams. When people asked what I did for a living, I would answer I owned a business, but quickly mention that it was small and only had a few part-time employees. When my parents laughed at the size of my business, it stung.

When you have an emotional reaction to money, whether it's yours or someone else's, it's important to dig deeper. What are your assumptions fueling those feelings? Is there any disconfirming evidence? If so, how can you rewrite your beliefs surrounding money?

Money Story 1: "I feel pathetic because I make less money than fresh college graduates."
Assumptions:
• Your salary should increase as you get older.
• Income determines your sense of life satisfaction and well-being.

Disconfirming Evidence:

- You work 1-2 days a week for that salary, so per hour, you're actually making more than you did as a college graduate. You've chosen to work less to focus on creative pursuits, so own the outcome!
- While money does increase subjective well-being, remember that you were closest to depression the year you made the most money.
- Your business allows you to live comfortably and the time to write this book, a life dream. Why are you not thrilled that you get to pursue this dream now?

Rewrite Belief:

- Money is an important factor for well-being, but not the only one. The past decade, I've prioritized freedom. I get to spend most of each day writing and hosting, which is what I would do if I had all the money in the world.

Money Story 2: "My friends make $250,000+ per year and I haven't cracked six figures. How have I fallen so far behind?"

Assumptions:

- Because you don't make as much money as your peers, you're a failure.

Disconfirming Evidence:

- Are those who make more money happier, healthier, fulfilled, and contributing more to society? Not necessarily. They are simply making more money, through a job or business that commands more value in the market. Are nurses, teachers and garbage collectors less essential than financiers?

Rewrite Belief:

- My business's revenue does not reflect my self worth. It reflects how much the market values my services. If I want to make more money, I can change my market and improve my service.
- Failure is not making less money than others. Failure is not having the courage to live a life true to myself; failure is not honoring my dreams and sharing my gift with others.

Money Story 3: "Money is evil"

Assumption:

- Rich people are greedy; money corrupts.

Disconfirming Evidence:

- The most generous and giving people you know are wealthy.
- People need money to survive, support their families and support others' livelihoods
- Money can further causes you value

Rewrite Belief:

- Money is good. With money, I can support myself, loved ones and the people and causes I believe in.

Deconstructing your beliefs might be the most important exercise in this book. You're writing your own script now! Over time, you begin shattering the limiting beliefs and unexamined assumptions that chain you down. Most of our scripts have been written by family and society. Don't let those scripts go unchecked. Humbly inquire to see if they are still valid for your life.

Financial goals are important, but if I fail to achieve them, I don't take it so personally. My skills and services may need to be improved, or I may need to change business models. But my worth as a human being has nothing to do with money. We must stand guard with our language about success and money.

Compare with Purpose & Accuracy

I should have been happy for Ethan, but honestly, all I felt was disbelief, and then jealousy. How did he sell his business for 1 million dollars? We had met five years ago in Vietnam when he had just started trying to make money online. He was a nice guy, but with a lot of questions too; I could never get much work done with him around. Somehow, he had cracked the code and created a million-dollar business while mine flatlined.

It's hard to avoid comparing yourself to others, especially with something as quantifiable as money. Purpose, impact and peace are much harder to measure! Research shows 10% of our daily thoughts involve making a comparison of some kind. Social media compounds our status-seeking - and suffering.

Here are some subject lines in my inbox:

- Student turned entrepreneur making $23 million/ year
- From customer support to $30,887,280
- Made 'redundant' at his job, he started a million-dollar, one-person business

It seems like everyone is making more money in one year on their first venture than I had in 10 years on multiple ventures. How could I not feel like a failure?

Comparing is inevitable. But I've learned to make healthier comparisons by making sure they are purposeful and accurate.

Does this comparison help you achieve your goals? (purpose)

What can I learn from the comparison that moves me closer to my goals? I try to avoid comparison for comparison's sake. That's like replaying your failures without learning the lesson.

I can learn so much from Ethan's experience: how he quickly found product-market fit, how he scaled his business, and how he secured financing to grow so fast. I try to make sure my comparisons have a purpose. Otherwise, it's unnecessary weight to carry.

Is your comparison realistic? (accuracy)

The average self-employed income in the US is around $48,000. Are you measuring yourself against outlier successes favored by the media? It's important to always look at the context surrounding a shiny number. I'm an optimist and a dreamer, but even so, why carry an unrealistic - and ultimately unhelpful - expectation of success? It would be much better to compare myself to, say, the top 10% of non-employer businesses, making $100,000 - $250,000, and then reminding myself that's a lofty goal, too.

Every week I'm flooded by emails, social media posts, and ads about fresh-faced entrepreneurs making millions. But they are certainly the exception. The one-person, one-million-dollar businesses covered by the media are the Olympic athletes of solopreneurs, comprising 0.3% of all non-employer businesses.

People start businesses for different reasons. If you value impact most, why are you comparing yourself to someone who values turning a quick dollar above all else? There are many lucrative businesses and markets that I'm not interested in or opposed to. Healthy comparisons need not just purpose, but accuracy too.

You Are Not Your Business

"Your business simply can't carry the weight of who you are - it will never be your value or your purpose. Nor is it a good love outlet, because it just can't love you back. Your start-up doesn't have the shoulders to bear that weight, and it shouldn't. So that misplaced emotional attachment has to go if you want to be healthy and strong for yourself, for your business, and for your family."

- Sherry Walling

Your creation is your baby. You give it your heart and soul. And then it fails.

You have no one else to blame.

With your livelihood, ego, and relationships at stake, it's no wonder that failing as an entrepreneur feels like death.

After many years of practice, I've developed a much healthier relationship with failure. I've accepted failure as part of the process - no businessman, creator or human being has a 100% success rate. Failure hurts like hell but is also my greatest teacher.

A business exists to solve a customer's problems.

That's it.

The problem is that we bring so much baggage to this equation. We run our businesses to prove someone wrong. We let our business results determine our self-worth. We expect customers to care because of our effort - instead of making something they value.

To this day, when I get a rude message from customers, I still get defensive. Even if only 1 out of 100 customers says something negative. Those notes stick for years. I take their criticism personally. How could I not? I've poured my heart and soul into providing them value, often for free.

But I've learned to pause, calm down, and separate the two. Don't take criticism personally. You are not your business.

If your product or service failed, it's a reflection of your business skills, offer and system, not your self worth.

It could also just be a hurt person lashing out. As Smart Passive Income's Pat Flynn wrote, "If someone is disrespectful and rude to you, don't pay any attention to him or her—they have deeper problems going on in their lives and they're taking it out on you." I've found this to be true. When I try to help these customers, they either don't reply or misunderstood our service.

Failure provides another data point for how you could serve your customers better.

Don't take it personally.

Learn. Adjust. Try again.

Nothing more, nothing less.

It's that simple.

When you separate yourself from your business, and strip your ego from the equation, you can see failure for what it is, whether that be a new insight about your customers, way to improve your decision making, or simply bad timing. And then jump back on your feet and move on.

The quicker you can see failure as feedback - and not the world conspiring against you or an indicator of your self-worth - the faster you can learn, adjust, try again, and eventually succeed. I've learned that this rate of change to meet market needs is far more indicative of business success than one's skill level or revenue. As a business owner, I most respect - and fear - competitors who learn and evolve quickly. We can decide whether to treat failure lightly, as information to learn from, or as an anchor that sinks us to the bottom of the ocean.

Another difficult lesson I've learned about business failure is that working hard does not guarantee business success. Many entrepreneurs who run or have sold businesses at substantial profit have told me the key to the game is staying in the game. Just give yourself enough chances to try again. I've heard this so many times: "I worked the same amount on this business as the few before, but this one just took off." Like pop artists, they can't explain why certain songs rocketed to the stratosphere and became smash hits. They just had to keep making songs.

Working hard might get you an A in school, but no amount of hard work will compensate for a service that doesn't help solve real customer problems.

Sherry Walling describes this as "start-up attachment disorder" - treating your startup like a lover and expecting it to love you back. It can't. Your business doesn't owe you anything.

This is easier said than done, but when failure strikes - and it will - I ask not, *Why is this happening to me?* but instead, *Why is this happening for me?*

Identifying with being instead of having attaches me less to the results. Instead, I ask what the results can teach me about being a better entrepreneur.

Be a Nobody

Business rejections are tough, but I find personal rejections even tougher. Nothing hurts more than when someone who captures your heart is not interested in you. The denial can be outright and direct, or agonizingly slow and subtle, but when the dust falls, you end up alone, heart-broken.

I used to wallow in self-pity for weeks, sometimes months, after a breakup. One time, as I told my best friend about the end of a relationship, I burst into tears, crying into a bowl of kimchi ji gae. That Korean restaurant became immortalized as "breakup cafe."

There are a surprising number of parallels between business failures and break-ups. They both crush the spirit. Some part of you just can't get over what should have been. We wallow in stubborn attachment to our desired alternative reality, complaining to our friends, and dragging out the drama by resenting and punishing those who turned us away.

What a waste of time. And what painful delusion.

The great American poet Maya Angelou had a rule, "When someone shows you who they are, listen."

Our ego, desires and attachments muddy our ability to see and experience reality. They make us force something that's simply not there for months - and sometimes years.

A tonic for failure - both business and personal - that has helped me is to remember Bruce Lee's paradoxical advice to *be a nobody*. One of the most iconic and ambitious movie stars of all-time, Lee wrote, "I must give up my desire to force, direct, strangle the world outside of me and the world within me in order to be completely open, responsible, aware and alive."

Being a nobody gives you the superpower of heightened awareness. Being a nobody allows you to respond naturally and easily, without all the rigmarole required to caress your ego. Being a nobody allows you to accept reality and "move like water, rest like a mirror, respond like an echo." Being a nobody puts you in your most fluid, unencumbered, effective state.

We need to stop fighting imaginary battles. Instead of fixating on what my ego craves and how someone or something should be, I can acknowledge what is:

She is sending clear signals about how she feels. You are not a priority for her. Time to let go and make room for women who like you. Thank her for her lessons. Drop the comfortable identity of being a victim. Wish her the best with her career and life.

As entrepreneurs, we are tenacious - and stubborn. It's difficult to know when to keep going and when to let go. But banging our heads against the same wall serves no one. Being a nobody helps us see the wall that doesn't need to be there. Yes, we must hold a strong vision for our lives. But equally important is remaining open to how we get there. The irony is that holding a view of our astounding insignificance is what allows us to achieve our limitless potential.

Identify Your Inner Critic

Failure can be instructive. But we must also learn to differentiate between the voice of constructive criticism and the destructive inner critic.

Constructive criticism isn't cruel, judgmental or punishing. It's a light, helpful voice:

- *You could do better. What could you do to improve?*
- *What could you put in as good effort?*
- *You made a mistake. Assess the situation, make a better decision and move on.*

The inner critic's voice undermines the goodness of our work and is harsh and prickly:

- *You always mess up.*
- *You're never prepared enough.*
- *You should have never started this project.*
- *You don't have it in you.*
- *You're never going to change.*

Any time you hear blanket, absolute statements made in damning fashion, pay attention. That's your inner critic. Would you say the same thing to a friend in a similar situation? Is this voice reasonable? Remember, your inner critic is yours, but it is not you.

Invoke a Protector

One of my favorite stories about overcoming doubt comes from the night of the Buddha's enlightenment.

As the Buddha meditates under the bodhi tree, the Demon Mara tries to distract him with temptations, but they fall to the ground as flowers. As a final attempt, Mara accuses the Buddha, "The seat you're sitting on is mine. I want it back." The Buddha reaches down, touches the Earth and proclaims, "The earth is my witness. I belong here." Mara shrinks away. The next morning, the Buddha gains enlightenment.

I love the symbolism of this story because doubt is often the fiercest - and last - obstacle before a breakthrough. Doubt paralyzes and prevents us from undertaking new and challenging experiences. And failure can make us doubt ourselves more. But we must remember, like Buddha, that this world is ours, and that we belong. I think Steve Jobs, founder of Apple, said it best: "Life can be much broader, once you discover one simple fact, and that is, everything around you that you call life was made up by people that were no smarter than you. And you can change it, you can influence it, you can build your own things that other people can use... Once you learn that, you'll never be the same again."

In Tibetan Buddhism, Buddha also invokes the protector deity, Mahakala, who sits on corpses and is surrounded by fire, to banish Mara as well. We sometimes need a protector, someone stronger than ourselves, to overcome the daggers of doubt.

Who is your protector, your Mahakala? Author Mimi Kuo-Deemer summons her father, circled around her infinitely, to banish doubt. The legendary American poet Maya Angelou invoked God to defend the clean, inviolate place inside her, that no one can curse, insult and treat with disrespect: "Back up! Not me you don't! Don't you know I'm a child of God?"

Who can you invoke to protect you against the demons of doubt? What ritual can remind you that you belong?

I hate to admit it, but sometimes during my entrepreneurial journey, I secretly wished that I loved finance so I could make millions like my friends. I could never be an investment banker, trader or bonds salesman. But damn, my friends who love this line of work are the lucky ones. They love work that paves a safer path to money, status and stability. Plus, they would not have to constantly defend themselves from their Asian parents.

Making a living working independently is not easy. Despite the start-up fairy tales you may see or hear, the vast majority of us have to confront instability and failure over and over again. We must accept that instability and failure are the costs of living a life of adventure and ingenuity. If you want financial stability and can't stomach failure, you should get a job.

That said, much of the instability we feel doesn't reflect reality. We carry having-based identities, unexamined money beliefs, and unhealthy comparisons, all unnecessary dead weight that hinders. We equate ourselves with our businesses and let our inner critic run amok, allowing failure to paralyze us instead of letting it guide us to create something more useful.

If your identity is having-based, you'll never be good enough - or at least be good enough for long. It's a precarious, stressful place to be. Being a self-employed, creative person is hard enough. Why not focus on being more of what you value and let go of the rest?

What's Your Perfect Day?
Finding Meaning on the Pathless Path

I'm packed in the subway commuting home.

After 20 minutes of avoiding touching others inches away, I squeeze out at Novena Station before the herd rushes in.

I emerge from the subway in a daze. The Singapore sun burns into me. As I walk home, my sweat spreads, tie-dyed, through my shirt. Just a hundred more meters. I grunt up the stairs, hurrying to open my door, eager to undress.

If this was an Olympic event, I'd be the world champion. He unbuttons his shirt in seconds! Look how he flings off the belt in one motion! And now for his signature move, the jump-out-of-the-pants. Mesmerizing! And the two sock-off-sit-down executed to perfection!

I lay like a blob on the couch, basking in my boxers, eyeing with disgust my slain (and crumpled) clothes.

Finally. Fucking. Free.

After 3 corporate jobs, I felt THE quiet desperation. Was this it? My tie felt like a noose; my starched shirt and stiff shoes a prison uniform. I yearned to be free.

That's when I read Timothy Ferriss's wildly popular *The 4-Hour Work Week*. It shook me to my core. This was the career script I had been looking for. Work from anywhere? Travel the world? Make more working less? Sign me up!

As I described in Chapter 2, the path was much more difficult. After quitting my job, it took me one year to make my first dollar. I spent another year throwing business ideas against the wall until one stuck - Touch MBA. It then took another 4 years of hard work before I had enough customers and processes in place that I could make as much as my last job (from six years ago!) working 2 days a week. That's years of watching your bank account drip away while your peers make six and seven figures from jobs - or businesses - they began at the same time.

At least I had won back 5 free days a week. I celebrated by exploring Vietnam. I took language classes. I moved to a beach town. I volunteered at youth leadership events around SouthEast Asia. Yet with all this freedom, all this independence, I'd end the days feeling lost and incomplete.

I was staring into the void.

1. "Am I really doing this to be more free and lead a better life, or am I just lazy?

2. Did I quit the rat race because it's bad, or just because I couldn't hack it? Did I just cop out?

3. Is this as good as it gets? Perhaps I was better off when I was following orders and ignorant of the possibilities. It was easier at least.

4. Am I really successful or just kidding myself?

5. Have I lowered my standards to make myself a winner? Are my friends, who are now making twice as much as three years ago, really on the right track?

6. Why am I not happy? I can do anything, and I'm still not happy. Do I even deserve it?"

Ferriss lists these six questions in the last chapter of *The 4-Hour Workweek*, "Filling the Void." The void, ironically, is the reward for building a 4-hour workweek business, and is full of "social isolation," "existential crises" and "frightening moments of doubt." Yikes!

Like every other first-time reader, I had skimmed this last chapter. The promise of working less from anywhere, to make more and live more, was too alluring. I would deal with the void and its big questions later.

Now I can see that filling the void is the most important chapter of the book. These six questions will plague you from start to finish. The void is both the prize and challenge of designing your life. I call it *the question*.

Tim's prescription is to enjoy more, learn more, and serve more.

Mine is to live your perfect day.

But first, let me get real with you.

The digital nomad lifestyle perks are real. Bringing your office in your backpack, and working when and where you want to - I've done it, and I've seen many good friends make a great living doing it, too. What's not shown is the lifestyle tax of *the question*.

The question is not the existential "What's the purpose of my life?" - although that is part of it.

The question is the uncertain, undefined and the gray. *The question* is a world of infinite possibility and options, where rules and definitions are bent, challenged, and sometimes disregarded. *The question* demands that you forge your own crutches of meaning to stand up in the face of massive uncertainty and ambiguity. In this life, there are no periods, only questions. There is no final answer.

We crave the flexibility of independent work, but be careful what you wish for - living with more options requires living with more energy, thought, and courage, too. Living with freedom requires a bigger battery and more processing power, because every day you're *living the question*. It has been the most challenging experience of my life.

President Barack Obama famously wore only two suits to avoid decision fatigue: "You need to routinize yourself. You can't be going through the day distracted by trivia." A number of notable business leaders stick with a signature look as well. Too much choice - and too many decisions - is taxing.

Imagine your life completely open ended. Where should you live? What should you work on? What's the best use of your time? Should you take a break? Do you even deserve one? It's tough to measure your progress when there are no easy markers of success. Meaning, adventure and impact are much harder to quantify than money. At least the rat race has clear finishing lines.

Add on top the massive uncertainty of starting a new venture. Is this the right business? The right product? The right price? Should you pivot? You're forever facing existential questions in business and life. That takes a toll.

Announcer (with cheesy game show voice): "*You're working for yourself. Congratulations! Here's your big, empty canvas. Go ahead, paint your masterpiece!*"

You: "*But what should I paint?*"

Announcer: "*Whatever youuuuu wantttttt!*"

While most fill in pre-drawn coloring books for their careers, you are staring at the blank page and wondering what crayons to use. Or if you should use crayons at all.

The tax of your freedom is having to deal with *the question* every day.

Falling into the void, I needed something to hang onto.

I needed to define my own rules for success and ground them in a daily practice. I needed to unearth what I truly valued. I needed a compass for this pathless path.

I found it in the perfect day.

The process is simple.

1. Imagine your perfect day.
2. Live it (or parts of it).
3. Score your day.

Why design your career - and combat the overwhelming freedom and uncertainty of independent work - through the frame of one day?

Your perfect day is easy to imagine. If you're like 40 people I've interviewed, you already know your perfect day in vivid detail. No soul searching or mind-altering substances required. You don't need to know the grand purpose of your life or have a 5, 10 and 25-year plan. And face it, those plans are just best guesses anyway. The Institute for the Future's panel of 20 technology, business and academic experts estimate that 85% of the jobs that today's learners will be doing in 2030 haven't been invented yet. Who knows what the world will look like in 10 years?

Your perfect day is actionable. Most career and self-help books exhort you to begin with the end in mind. It is difficult - dare I say impossible? - to see so far into the future. Meanwhile, you are constantly evolving as a person and professional, so by the time you arrive, that big vision of yours will likely be outdated. So instead of guessing what you should do and who you want to be years from now, why not make today your masterpiece?

From Life Purpose to Perfect Day

- From *What do I want to do with my life?* to *How do I want to spend the day?*
- From *What impact do I want to make?* to *Who can I impact today?*
- From *What do I want people at my funeral to say about me?* to *How can I help someone today?*

You're much closer to who you are tomorrow than who you will be in five years. By living your perfect day now, you can build your way forward into a life that thrills and fulfills you, each step of the way.

If you want to be an artist, entrepreneur, or social worker, ask those people about their average day. What do they do, who do they work with, and what do they love and hate about it? What are their day's biggest challenges? Does that day get you excited? That's a much better way to evaluate a career than pursuing a path solely because of monetary status or lifestyle perks.

Your perfect day is measurable. At the end of each day, observe what you did and rank your day. What affected your score? Soon enough, you will recognize what truly fulfills you and makes you optimistic about the future.

What's Your Perfect Day?

So, what is your perfect day?

Find a quiet and expansive space and give yourself 10 minutes to be completely present. It's important that you feel calm and relaxed – not rushed.

No thinking is required! Just notice what first comes to mind. Jot down notes if you'd like. Don't limit yourself. After all, it's your perfect work day. There is no way you can fail. And you have the time, money and resources to do whatever you want.

The following questions have helped me see my perfect day with more clarity:

- What would you wake up most excited to do on your perfect day?
- What are you doing and when?

- Where are you?
- Who are you with?
- What does your perfect day feel like?
- What values would guide your perfect day?
- What would not be a part of your perfect day?
- What needs to be released for your perfect day to manifest?
- What needs to be embraced for your perfect day to manifest?
- Now that you've spent a few minutes thinking about this, what else wants to be known about your perfect day?

After you've completed the questions, write about the images, thoughts and feelings that came into your awareness. Allow them to formulate into a sense of personal direction.

WHAT'S YOUR PERFECT DAY?

WHEN & WHAT?	WITH WHO?	HOW DOES IT FEEL?

WHAT MUST YOU EMBRACE?	WHAT MUST YOU LET GO?

Secret Wishes

What did you realize about your perfect day?

Living the question overwhelmed me in 2017. I couldn't find the answers through my usual method of reading books. I realized that 90% of my books were written by white, male entrepreneurs from western societies. Most of the thinkers I admired shared a similar worldview. Where could I find different ideas about the good life?

Maybe the answers were right in front of me. I couldn't think of anything else, so I started asking friends and strangers in Vietnam about their perfect day.

Rich or poor, young or old, manual laborer or office worker – it didn't matter. I wanted to learn from a broader spectrum of lived experience. I had idolized the rich, famous and powerful. Maybe the average man or woman had something to teach me.

I've asked dozens of people about their perfect day.

Many times, I heard opinions:

- "People should do ___"
- "Stoics believed that ___"
- "This expert says we should do ___"

I tried to move people from others' opinions to their own experience, from their minds to their hearts. I wanted their answers to well up from deep inside them, and I wanted to feel their energy expand.

- From "People should do ___" to "How does doing ___ make you feel?"
- From "Stoics believed that ___" to "How do you make ___ part of your perfect day?"
- From "This expert says we should do ___" to "Tell me about a time when you did ___"

Your perfect day should resonate through your entire being and fascinate you. It should fill you with joy and excitement like a secret wish.

Keep going until you feel this way.

Example: Darren's Perfect Day

- **Wake up** rested, surrounded by nature, with a prayer of gratitude. Get outside and feel cool, fresh air. Light walk or qigong to stretch, move, and get blood circulating. With: alone. Feels: calm, clean, clear.
- **Nutritious breakfast & coffee.** With: significant other. Feels: invigorating.
- **Mornings** dedicated to creative, deep work: writing, hosting, brainstorming new content, prod-

ucts, plans, conceived in a quiet, soaring, inspiring setting. With: alone. Feels: creative, focused, important.

- **Healthy lunch** with inspirational people that brighten the world. With: masters of their craft. Feels: full of growth and possibility, re-energizing.
- **Afternoons** dedicated to people: attracting and developing world-class talent, cultures and systems that enable people to do their best work. With: partners, mentors, mentees, customers, employees. Feels: connected, impactful, magnified
- **Early evening** outside as the sun sets, playing sports or practicing a physical skill where I enter the flow state. With: hobby friends, practitioners, competitors. Feels: present, physical, fun.
- **Delicious dinner** with loved ones, sharing stories, struggles and laughs. With: family, friends. Feels: grateful, joyful.
- **After dinner** entertainment and reading, exploring new worlds, people and interests. With: creators, family, friends. Feels: magical.
- **Bedtime** close connection. With: significant other. Feels: intimate, open, spent (in a good way).

- **What must you embrace?** Earlier mornings, fresh starts.

- **What you must let go?** Toxic people, food and environments.

....

What I Learned from Asking 40 People about Their Perfect Day

While everyone's perfect day is unique, I've found they tend to share similar characteristics.

I had no expectations. If anything, I yearned to hear wildly different ideas about their perfect day. Yet after 40 conversations, I've found that people mostly want four things: connection, autonomy, progress and a peaceful state of mind.

Below, I define these four terms and share direct quotes from my conversations. Are these part of your perfect day?

Connection: spending time with close friends or loved ones

- "For me, a perfect day is when I catch some fish to bring back to my grandma. It would make me proud." (Sparky, Vietnam)
- "I got to spend it with people I love." (Ramon, USA)
- "A small group of friends having fun and telling stories in a safe setting." (JJ, Ireland)

Autonomy: having control over your day

- "I can do whatever I want, whenever I want, spend whatever I want, and be with whoever I want." (Grace, Hong Kong)
- "I would love to rest and spend time doing things I love." (Linh, Vietnam)
- "My perfect day is free form, not feeling rushed at any point, just being free to go… I literally have space and time to approach the day." (Rebecca, USA)

Progress: getting better at something or getting important things done

- "Having the feeling of achieving something." (Manuel, Germany)
- "I have to dance until I reach a feeling: 'Yeah, I'm good.' It's a release, a deeply soulful activity to me. That's a perfect day." (Jimmy, USA)
- "When I come back home, I feel very tired – a good feeling tired – and I'm happy the day was spent the way it was spent." (Maud, France)

Peaceful State of Mind: entering a flow state or having a clear mind absent of anxiety

- "When I forget that I exist, I feel like I'm my best self." (Shane, Singapore)
- "Every day is perfect because I am alive." (Convenience store clerk, Vietnam)

- "If I have no issues at work and no issues in my personal life, that's a perfect day. My mind is sober and very clear." (Chung, Taiwan)

I was shocked to see these four elements appear again and again, no matter the age, sex, nationality, and socioeconomic status of my interviewees.

Edward Deci and Richard Ryan's self-determination theory, developed over 40 years and backed by hundreds of studies, found that humans have an innate psychological need to be autonomous, competent, and connected to one another.

This matched well with what friends and strangers in Vietnam were telling me about their perfect day: feeling a sense of control, effectiveness, and connectedness. When those three needs are satisfied, we're motivated, productive and happy. When they're thwarted, our wellness plummets.

So, whenever I feel overwhelmed by *the question*, I think about these three elements. Usually I'm missing one or two, and the result is that I feel isolated, blocked or directionless. I troubleshoot my day with three questions:

1. Are you getting better at something you value?
2. Are you spending time with close friends and loved ones?

3. Are you making time for things that give you a peaceful state of mind?

Three questions that I hope help you design your perfect day.

Score Your Day

After imagining and living your perfect day, you must score it.

As a kid, my tennis coach would tell me: "After you hit a winner, stop and remember what it felt like. Replay the shot in your mind. What did it sound like? What was your footwork? How did your body feel? What were you thinking to strike the ball that way?"

I would replay the shot and relive the feeling in my mind. I'd hit the same backhand from my point of view, from my opponent's point of view, and from the imaginary TV cameras above. The goal? To create a well-worn groove to access that same state in the future. After practice, I'd record these feelings in a notebook.

This brief pause to stop, observe, and view your situation from multiple vantage points, and course-correct is the final pillar of your perfect day.

We need to quickly review our day and externalize what made it great while we can still remember what we did and what the day felt like. *What did this amazing day feel like? What made it that way? How could you design this to happen again with greater ease?*

Or on the flip side: *Why did this day suck? What did it feel like? What could you do differently tomorrow to avoid a day like this?*

At the end of each day, I fill out my "DJ Daily," a form that reminds me of what's important and whether I'm headed in the right direction.

The "DJ Daily" anchors me to daily practices that I've realized make me feel great about the day. The form takes less than three minutes to complete.

....

Example: DJ Daily

"Yesterday is but a dream, and tomorrow is only a vision. But today well lived makes every yesterday a dream of happiness, and every tomorrow a vision of hope." - Kalidasa

2020 Goals
- Test business ideas with million dollar market potential
- Be the healthy, loving long-term partner you desire
- Get 1,000 true fans for ASE Podcast

Fourth Quarter Goals for 2020

- Launch minimum viable product
- Invest in a therapist
- Finish writing book

Daily Questions

1. Did you treat your mind to a 5-minute meditation? (yes/no)
2. Did you treat your body to a 15-minute sweat, workout or stretch with your undivided attention? (yes/no)
3. Did you visualize your best life to 1 song? (yes/no)
4. What most important task did you work on related to your 2020 goals? (fill in the blank)
5. Did you do your best to connect with loved ones or inspiring people? (yes/no)
6. Did you do your best to have fun, play, and relax? (yes/no)
7. Did you do your best to help someone today? Gifts and random acts of kindness are cool. (yes/no) If so, who and how? (fill in the blank)
8. What did you do today? (fill in the blank)
9. Score your day (-2 = horrible day, -1 = bad day, 0 = okay, 1 = good day, 2 = fantastic day)

10. Why did you score your day so? (fill in the blank)

See the form at bit.ly/djdaily

....

SCORING YOUR DAY

DAILY REVIEW FORM

- DID YOU... ? (yes/no)
- DID YOU... ? (yes/no)
- DID YOU... ? (yes/no)

PUT +1 and +2 ACTIVITIES HERE

- WHAT DID YOU DO TODAY? _____

- SCORE YOUR DAY?   (-2 = horrible day, -1 = bad day, 0 = okay, +1 = good day, +2 = fantastic day)

- WHY DID YOU SCORE YOUR DAY SO? _____

If 10 questions are too much for you, I believe much of the value can be captured in the last two questions:

- Score your day (-2 = horrible day, -1 = bad day, 0 = okay, 1 = good day, 2 = fantastic day)
- Why did you score your day so?

Do this enough times and your criteria for a great day will become increasingly obvious. You start structuring your day to give yourself the best chance of scoring a 1 or 2. *The question* never goes away but will consume less of your mental resources. Over time, you begin to routinize activities that lead to a good day. Like Barack Obama wearing only two suits, you'll discover a handful of "perfect day templates" that allow you to perform and feel great about your day - without all the decision fatigue.

The perfect day is really about exploring one question: What has to happen for you to feel good about your day?

This will be different for everyone and change over time. But through a 10-minute visualization and daily score, you can start writing your own playbook. Each day you gain a clearer understanding of what's important to you and calibrate your work-life compass.

We all want to be the fastest man in the world. But have you seen Usain Bolt's daily practices, sprinting on an empty track in the scorching afternoon sun? He calls it "The work behind the scenes." The perfect day is about figuring out what you love to do behind the scenes - without the results, accolades and trappings of success. It's about understanding what makes you smile before bed, because you spent your day on the people, activities and causes that fulfill you. It's the best tool I've found to navigate the void and chart your own path with confidence.

Who Are You Grooming?
Dunbar & Dealing with Loneliness

I look out onto Tuyen Lam lake in Dalat, a stunning scene in Vietnam. The wind ripples through the water, a shimmering glass that reflects the hills of pine trees above. I sip my hot Americano, close my eyes, and bask in the late morning sun. I'm not the only one enjoying this rare January treat. Three dogs lay sideways in front of me, breathing deeply, eyes half-open, soaking in this bliss.

It's Wednesday morning. While most hurried to work, I strolled to my favorite breakfast spot for bánh mì xíu mại and sữa đậu nành before motorbiking through the hills to arrive here. It's a dream morning - delicious food, easy adventure, and discovery of hidden treasure.

I am also alone.

My dance friends and I traveled to Dalat to celebrate the New Year. We ate hot pot, toured the town, and danced till 5am in our villa. But they returned to Ho Chi Minh City on Sunday to start the work week.

When I quit my job, my goal was to have mornings like this. No morning rush hour. No drab office and office clothes. Just complete control over the pace and space of day. It still is thrilling a decade later, this total freedom to choose my day.

It can also be isolating. I don't care how many stunning lakes, beaches, or cityscapes you choose as your office, how many countries you visit, or how much amazing creative work you do. If you're alone and just doing it for yourself, the perks start to feel meaningless.

I'll return to this idyllic cafe to soak in the majestic lake and breathe the crisp mountain air. But I'll also fly back to bustling Ho Chi Minh City in a few days to be with friends for the weekend. While I cherish my freedom of time and mobility, I've learned that I value relationships and rooted-ness within a community even more.

We evolved as social animals. To survive working alone, we need to reinstall ancient tribal structures. Your tribes might look drastically different than they do now. But they are essential to your success and well-being as you chart your own path. I enjoy solo getaways for periods of time, but not the long run. Too long and I feel a withering away, despite the once-in-a-lifetime adventure. I'm convinced that few can survive this path alone.

I would like to share four practices I've found most helpful to combat loneliness and isolation being self-employed.

Find a New Inner Circle & Superfamily

While studying correlations between primates' neocortex sizes and group sizes, Robin Dunbar, an anthropologist, theorized that human beings could cognitively maintain roughly 150 casual friendships. "Dunbar's Number" has been used to explain the average group size of hunter-gatherer societies (148.4) and company sizes of professional armies throughout history (100-200).

But I focus on Dunbar's "rule of 3," that shows human social groups are often hierarchically structured in series of 3-5 (inner circle - closest support group), 9-15 (superfamily - intimates you can confide in), 30-45 (clan - friends you'd invite to a dinner party), and then 100-150 (tribe - casual friendships). I find it miraculous that these concentric group sizes have followed me through every stage of life, from grade school to my independent working life now.

That nucleus of 3-5 people would usually be your partner, family and best friends – those you seek in times of trouble.

The challenge is that sometimes your partner, family and best friends can't see you as an entrepreneur. As my parents still say ten years in, "Darren, get a job!"

Pursuing your perfect day can often conflict with those closest to you. This is one of the most difficult challenges of charting your own path. As if starting a business wasn't hard enough. You often find yourself isolated from those whose support you crave the most.

That's why you must find a new inner circle where you can openly share your challenges, get outside perspective, and find emotional support. Masterminds, discussed in Chapter 2 and 3, are one solution. You find 3-5 other solopreneurs to share, advise, and keep you accountable. Getting fresh perspectives on your business is game-changing. Equally important is finding those few longtime friends who support you being your own boss, with whom you can share your struggles.

I keep a spreadsheet with each of these groups:

- Inner Circle (3-5 people) - contact every 15 days
- Superfamily (15 people) - contact every 30 days
- Clan (50 people) - contact every 90 days
- Tribe (150 people) - contact every 180 days

Their names turn red if I haven't contacted them within the designated time periods. I set aside a few hours every Friday afternoon to proactively stay in touch. How do you feel about people who only contact you when they need something? Being a good friend or community member means helping, contributing and looking to add value before you need anything.

After many Fridays doing this, I've realized nurturing 150 relationships is not easy. So, if time is short, I focus on the 20 people in my inner circle and superfamily. I make sure they are people I absolutely love spending time with, who are hubs to other networks of amazing people. Am I in touch and can I help them? These are your support circles to lean on in tough times. It's the best investment you can make to cope with the emotional challenges of working alone.

Throughout history, we would see members of our tribe every day. Today, social media gives us the illusion that we are in touch with those who mean the most. Do an audit. When was the last time you connected with those in your inner circle and superfamily? Half of those people, for me, aren't on social media. I need a list to remind me every week about who matters most.

Monkeys, humanity's closest kin, groom each other to make friends, cement bonds, and influence other primates. Dunbar theorized that humans developed language to "groom" a larger number of tribe members. So every time I connect with members of my tribe, I imagine myself metaphorically brushing their fur. Touch matters. And if you can't physically touch those closest to you, try your best to simulate touch through your words, outreach and actions. The troop that grooms together, stays together.

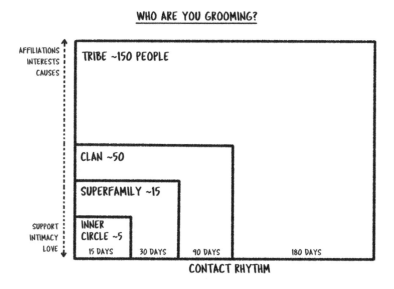

to simulate touch through your words, outreach and actions. The troop that grooms together, stays together.

WHO ARE YOU GROOMING?

Join Tribes that Serve a Bigger Purpose

I'll admit that after 10 years of working on my own, there have been times when I've wanted to get a job just to be with people. Sure, a salary, benefits and new skills would be fantastic. But just to be with others - that's the real draw.

When I quit my last job in 2011 I never thought I would say that. I cherished quiet, creative mornings. I hated clocking in and out and dealing with office politics.

But I've realized that working completely on our own goes against our nature as humans. We crave to belong and be of value to a community. And when you exist outside that structure, life can feel meaningless.

As an independent worker, you must find a practicing community of peers. Finding a group of peers going through similar challenges - and whom you can help and learn from - is empowering and necessary for survival. It has never been easier to find communities and events full of people who share your interests - and if you can't find one, organize your own!

Second, can you use your flexibility and freedom to support the causes and communities closest to your heart? I've spent most of the past year writing this book - a life dream which I hope helps the growing number of free-lancers, creators and solopreneurs manage their mental and emotional well-being. When my Dad needed emergency heart surgery, I was able to fly from Colombia to California the next day to be with him for months. And being part of basketball and salsa communities wherever I am in the world has done more for my physical, emotional and mental well-being than anything else. So, double down on your life's hobbies, causes and interests. That will help anchor meaning into your new way of working.

Ideally, the work you choose fulfills you not just financially, but emotionally, mentally and spiritually. But I understand that is not always the case. That's why it's so important to proactively nurture community outside of our businesses.

Interests & Mastery Shrink the World

We've all been to dreadful networking events, passing out business cards and making surface-level conversation soon forgotten. Forced socialization is awkward and painful - and I'm an extrovert. Networking to network almost never works.

The best networking strategy is to be excellent at what you love to do. As Dan Andrews, organizer of the influential Dynamite Circle network, often says, "Network is a multiplier." Meeting people is easiest - and more powerful - when can you offer something of value.

So, instead of networking, pursue your passions, interests and causes with reckless abandon, and find (or start) groups of people doing the same. You'll meet fascinating people, and your friendships will grow organically.

My friend Jimmy has been teaching salsa for nearly 20 years. He lives and breathes the music, culture and history of the dance. Every day, he dances for hours, entering a flow state to connect with Orishas - the deities worshipped by the Yoruba people in West Africa whose culture form the roots of salsa. I joined his park workouts, and we started a club - 239Boyz, named after our 23/9 park - focused on calisthenics, afro-cuban dancing and salsa.

At first, there were just a few of us, dancing shirtless to the African drums. We always had some curious onlookers. We were, after all, dancing African folklore in Vietnam. But soon, a few more joined in, and then more. After 18 months, there are 50 people in our group, all passionate about fitness and the roots of salsa dance. We've performed together, partied together, and gone on retreats together. For many of us, it's our primary group of friends in Vietnam. Members call each other brother, sister and often refer to the 239Boyz as "family."

It has also been an easy and fun way to meet people of all different nationalities, professions, genders and ages. Our love for dancing binds us together. Members support each other's businesses and families. And we meet 3-4 times a week to practice, more than most people meet their closest friends. No wonder we feel so close to each other.

Our social circles used to revolve around family, work and religion. As more people live apart from family and work on their own, they will seek communion with new families. People like Jimmy are the new priests of this modern world, bringing people together in service of a greater cause. Organizers of real and virtual communities are incredibly valuable and powerful. Whether for dance, board games, or digital marketing, I've seen how much of a difference weekly, monthly, and annual gatherings can make in people's lives.

I never knew how many interesting people I'd meet through tennis. Competing since age eight, I considered tennis war. It was only after university that I realized how many different circles welcomed me because I was a skilled tennis player. I've met mentors, entertainers and moguls just because I was top 10% in the world at something.

It's much easier to meet people through a shared interest when the focus is on doing something, not meeting people. People can let go of titles and status and just be themselves. I'll often find out someone's job a year or two after meeting them. The key is to find interest groups you are proud to affiliate with and contribute to them. Get better at what you love to do. If you can't find these communities, start them yourself.

Adventure together, master together, compete together, and build something together - those are the friendships you'll remember at the end of your life.

Invest in Friends

"Even if we have a lot of money in the bank, we can die very easily from our suffering. So, investing in a friend, making a friend into a real friend, building a community of friends, is a much better source of security. We will have someone to lean on, to come to, during our difficult moments."

- Thich Nhat Hanh

When I read the quote above, I was skeptical. Really? Investing in friends is a much better source of security than money?

Five close friends would be nice to have... but five million dollars? Now that's security!

Yet after achieving my highest income ever in 2017, I felt isolated, lost and anxious – the exact opposite of Merriam-Webster's definition of security: "The state of feeling safe, stable, and free from fear or anxiety." How could this be?

Investing in money or friends is a false dichotomy – of course, we want both and should invest in both. The real question is whether you'd take less money for better relationships or sacrifice close relationships for more money.

I define security as living a long, healthy, happy life. What will make me feel safe, stable and free from fear or anxiety now and in the future? In addition to living and scoring my perfect day, I've looked to outside studies to help me answer this question. This way, I can benefit from the collective wisdom of thousands of lives. While this section is about investing in relationships, I think we must also consider money's importance for security in parallel.

Money Matters for Well-Being

The Cantril Self-Anchoring Striving Scale, pioneered in 1965, has been used by a wide variety of researchers in more than 150 countries to assess well-being.

> "Please imagine a ladder with steps numbered from zero at the bottom to 10 at the top. The top of the ladder represents the best possible life for you, and the bottom of the ladder represents the worst possible life for you.
>
> On which step of the ladder would you say you personally feel you stand at this time?
>
> On which step do you think you will stand about five years from now?"

Research across the world indicates substantial correlations between the Cantril Scale and income. Gallup formed three statistically relevant groups to help explain results: "thriving" (life evaluations of 7 and above), "struggling" (5-6), and "suffering" (4 and below). The percentage "thriving" across countries correlates highly with per-capita GDP, and the percent "suffering" correlates highly with other measures of poverty. Respondents with lower incomes were more likely to report lacking food and shelter, having physical pain, stress, worry sadness and anger. For example, the percent "suffering" is less than 1% in Denmark and 40% in Zimbabwe.

Betsey Stevenson and Justin Wolfers have compared well-being across countries, across several different surveys, and found that there is no satiation point beyond which money doesn't increase subjective well-being. This strong relationship between income and subjective well-being holds for both rich and poor countries.

Other studies, most notably by Nobel prize-winning duo Angus Deaton and Daniel Kahneman, have concluded that higher incomes improve evaluation of life but not emotional well-being beyond an annual income of $75,000 USD (90,000 USD today). Nevertheless, it remains clear that up to a certain point, income is correlated with well-being.

More money – and living in richer, more developed countries – is strongly correlated with life satisfaction and well-being. Making money and building economically valuable skills should be a top priority for well-being.

But Financial Independence Can Also Lead to Isolation

Ironically, it was during my highest earning months that I was the closest to depression. I would work online, alone in cafes all day, and return to an empty apartment. I depended on no one, and no one depended on me. Sometimes I would go a week without seeing anyone.

I could travel anywhere, but I was tired of traveling alone. I could work anywhere but cringed at the thought of rebuilding life in another country. I had achieved digital nomad nirvana but found myself asking, what for?

Filmmaker and anthropologist Sebastian Junger sums this up beautifully in his book *Tribe: On Homecoming and Belonging*:

> "According to a global survey by the World Health Organization, people in wealthy countries suffer depression at as much as eight times the rate they do in poor countries... The mechanism seems simple: poor people are forced to share their time and resources more than wealthy people are, and as a result, they live in closer communities. Inter-reliant poverty comes with its own stresses—and certainly isn't the American ideal—but it's much closer to our

evolutionary heritage than affluence. A wealthy person who has never had to rely on help and resources from his community is leading a privileged life that falls way outside more than a million years of human experience. Financial independence can lead to isolation, and isolation can put people at a greatly increased risk of depression and suicide. This might be a fair trade for a generally wealthier society—but a trade it is."

Junger argues that humans have evolved over millions of years through group survival, especially to share food and for self-defense. I had invested everything into my business, which provided income and freedom. But who was I helping to feed and defend? No one. Despite my success, I had never felt more lonely.

Lean Into Relationships

Many studies show that relationships are central to emotional wellness and longevity.

The Harvard Study of Adult Development is one of the longest running studies on adult life, tracking 724 poor and privileged men since they were teenagers in 1938 – over 80 years ago! Every two years, these men were asked questions about their lives and mental and emotional wellness.

"The surprising finding is that our relationships and how happy we are in our relationships has a powerful influence on our health," said Robert Waldinger, the fourth director of the study. "Our study has shown that the people who fared the best were the people who leaned into relationships with family, with friends and with community."

The study found that close relationships, more than money or fame, are what keep people happy throughout their lives. Relationships protect people from hardship, help delay mental and physical decline, and are better predictors of long and happy lives than social class, IQ, or genes.

Researchers Julianne Holt-Lunstad and Timothy B. Smith sought to determine the extent to which social relationships influence mortality risk, and which aspects of social relationships matter most. After looking at multiple studies across 308,849 individuals, they concluded that individuals with adequate social relationships have a 50% greater likelihood of survival compared to those with poor or insufficient social relationships. The magnitude of having stronger social relationships is comparable with quitting smoking and exceeds other risk factors for mortality such as obesity and physical inactivity. They identified close relationships (i.e. having friends you know will support you in bad times) and social integration (i.e. interactions with people as you move through your day) as important predictors of longevity.

National Geographic explorer Dan Buettner and a team of researchers studied regions with a high percentage of healthy centenarians - what they termed Blue Zones. They found that the world's longest lived, happiest people prioritize relationships, through belonging to faith-based communities, putting loved ones first, and choosing social circles that support healthy behaviors.

One of my favorite stories from Blue Zones is the Okinawan concept of "moai:" a small group of lifelong friends. Moais start in childhood and extend into the 100s. Forming a second family, moai members meet regularly and support each other socially and financially. As one 77-year old moai member shared, "Each member knows that her friends count on her as much as she counts on her friends. If you get sick or a spouse dies or if you run out of money, we know someone will step in and help. It's much easier to go through life knowing there is a safety net."

Bronnie Ware spent several years as a palliative nurse caring for patients in the last weeks of their lives. She realized that the dying shared five common regrets, all of which are touched on in this book! One common regret of the dying was wishing they had stayed in touch with friends.

1. "I wish I'd had the courage to live a life true to myself, not the life others expected of me.
2. I wish I hadn't worked so hard.
3. I wish I'd had the courage to express my feelings.

4. I wish I had stayed in touch with my friends.

5. I wish that I had let myself be happier."

The Harvard Study of Adult Development, Blue Zone study, and our evolutionary history point towards investing in relationships for a longer, healthier and happier life. We have evolved by depending on relationships; without contributing to a tribe, we wither.

Financial advisors teach us to diversify our investments across and within asset classes to reduce risk and volatility. In other words, don't put all your eggs into one basket.

Why not take a similar approach to investing in friends?

Below is a checklist for auditing your investments in friends. I try to cultivate these relationships before I need anything:

- Friends you can count on in an emergency
- Friends with whom you can share your deepest struggles and joys
- With which three people do you spend the most time? Do their habits make you happier and healthier? If not, with whom should you spend more time?
- Small, support groups of mutual interest
- Communities that feed and protect what is most important to you

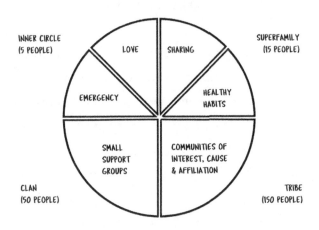

When I think of security, my mind cuts to scenes from insurance and banking commercials. A montage of falling in love, buying a house, sending a kid to college, living to a golden age, and of course, meeting an advisor in a suit. It ends with the man looking back on life, fulfilled. He provided for his family. The message? Security is being wise with your finances.

Security is never portrayed as having a close circle of friends, healthy lifestyle, and everyday purpose within a community. But most research points to precisely these things for a happy, healthy, long life. Imagine these scenes instead: visiting a friend at the hospital, walking in nature with a loved one, babysitting a grandkid, building a school.

A fulfilling and secure life comes from prioritizing loved ones and community.

Ten years on this journey has taught me that relationships are my most important assets. Reflecting upon and scoring each day, I've learned that if I have to make a tradeoff between money and friends, I should invest in relationships. A day spent with loved ones and inspiring people is never a negative day and often predicts whether I score it a 1 or 2. And studying thousands of lives suggests that relationships are likelier to help me feel happier, healthier and live longer.

Living the Questions

"Be patient toward all that is unsolved in your heart and to try to love the questions themselves like locked rooms and like books that are written in a very foreign tongue. Do not now seek the answers, which cannot be given you because you would not be able to live them. And the point is, to live everything. Live the questions now. Perhaps you will then gradually, without noticing it, live along some distant day into the answer."

- Rainer Maria Rilke

The solopreneurship life is thrilling. Never before have so many people had the opportunity to design their careers - and perfect days. People can now make a great living entirely on their own, working from anywhere.

We see digital nomads living wild and free, laptops and coffees in front of stunning scenery all around the world. And if you want to jump on this train, there is no shortage of books, courses and communities that promise millions and the lifestyle. The upside.

Surviving this path for 10 years has taught me something different. That the most important thing you can do is protect against the downside. Failure, anxiety, instability and loneliness (FAIL) should be expected and planned for. We must make self-employment FAIL-safe so that we consistently return to a safe, stable condition after the inevitable breakdowns. If you can manage the rollercoaster of entrepreneurship, creative work and working on your own, you will not only be able to offer more value to the world, but also reap the benefits of your new flexible work-life.

The problem is no one likes to talk about the downsides. It's not fun to read about failure, stress, instability, and loneliness. No one wants to throw the wet blanket on others' dreams.

Making money is challenging, but even more demanding is managing your physical, mental and emotional well-being. Solopreneurship takes an enormous toll on all three. To survive this path, you need to stay in the game. And to stay in the game, your well-being deserves just as much care and attention as your business.

At the beginning of the book, I mentioned the Four Horsemen. Now you have tools to deal with all four.

WORK-LIFE VALUE - COST

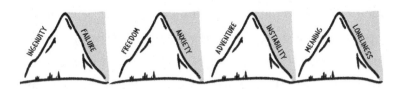

Ingenuity <> Failure

- What's your shadow? (Practice 1)
- How are you the master of your disaster? (Practice 1)
- Own your entire story (Practice 1)
- Experiment with new activities, ways of being and relationships (Practice 2)
- You are not your business (Practice 5)
- Be a nobody (Practice 5)
- Identify your inner critic (Practice 5)
- Invoke a protector (Practice 5)

Freedom <> Anxiety

- Love yourself when you feel scared, angry or ashamed (Practice 1)
- Take time off seriously (Practice 3)

- Problem-based coping (Practice 3)
- Emotion-based coping (Practice 3)
- Guardrails (Practice 3)
- Who keeps you accountable? (Practice 3)
- What's your perfect day? (Practice 5)

Adventure <> Instability

- Make it easy to win (Practice 2)
- Make it safer to play (Practice 2)
- To have or to be? (Practice 4)
- Examine your money beliefs (Practice 4)
- Compare with purpose and accuracy (Practice 4)
- You are not your business (Practice 5)
- Invest in friends (Practice 6)

Meaning <> Loneliness

- Make it bigger than you (Practice 2)
- Choose environments that hold the space for your desired identity (Practice 2)
- Mastermind challenges (Practice 2)
- What's your perfect day? (Practice 5)
- Score your day (Practice 5)
- Find a new inner circle and superfamily (Practice 6)
- Join tribes that serve a bigger purpose (Practice 6)
- Interests and mastery shrink the world (Practice 6)
- Invest in friends (Practice 6)

Charting your own path will require more of you than anything you've ever done - more courage, energy, and resilience. You must write your own rules of success, face your demons, and own the outcomes. You must embrace living the questions and get comfortable walking a path with no easy answers and no finish line.

What has worked for me is to own the duality of my story, personality and the self-employed life, and to walk the middle path. There are always two sides to the coin; opposites need each other to exist. Acknowledging this is the starting point. I grew up performing to please my parents and win their affection, which has made me who I am today: a diligent worker and people person still too dependent on others for affirmation. The flip sides to my abundant curiosity, spontaneity, and enthusiasm are a difficulty focusing, poor practical skills and a stubborn independence. So I must learn to manage these assets and liabilities. And I hope I've convinced you to expect not just the upsides but also the downsides of pursuing a work-life full of freedom, adventure and meaning. We must acknowledge the light and dark of ourselves, others and every situation.

We choose this path for the freedom. But ironically, we need others to stay on the path because surviving solo is damn near impossible. We need to re-institute tribal structures and outside accountability to stay productive, sane, and to gain much needed perspective. This makes the journey both easier and more meaningful.

If you're looking for more resources that can help you manage your well-being while being your own boss, go to upstartist.tv.

I wish you well-being on your entrepreneurial journey. The world needs you at your best!

Acknowledgements

I would first like to thank my grandparents and parents who worked so hard to give me the opportunities that led to this book. Thank you for doing all you could to help me. I am so fortunate for winning this lottery. Thank you, Mom and Dad. I love you.

Thank you to John Kaaiohelo, Matt Fujieki, and Matt McGarvey for encouraging me to write this book. And a loving nod to my brother, Jason Joe, who has silently supported me from afar. This would never have gotten off the ground without you band of brothers.

Thank you to Dr. Carl Jung, Dr. Erich Fromm, Dr. Herminia Ibarra, and Dr. Sherry Walling for your life's work, which form the foundation of this book. Thank you to Ricardo Semler, Jon Jandai, Derek Sivers, Mimi-Kuo Deemer, Sebastian Junger, and Charles Eisenstein for boldly asking why and living out your lives of radical wisdom. You are my inspirations.

Thank you to my salsa family in Vietnam - James Yoon, Dai Nguyen, Natasha Yeh, Bachir Mets, and Nadia Waridi - for supporting me and lifting my spirit every time I see you. Thank you to my first readers - John Kaaiohelo, Matt Fujieki, Lana Sher, Jennifer Yeh Wannenmacher, David

Hehenberger, Hui Ying Chin and Nadia Waridi - for your invaluable perspective that helped shape so much of this book. You've held the space for me to be an author, and I couldn't have finished the book without you.

Finally, thank you to the people of Vietnam, who have taught me that a life full of relationships is a rich one.

About the Author

Darren C. Joe quit his last job in 2011 and has since been self-employed. After working as a business analyst in the shipping and publishing industries and then as an MBA Admissions Director, he started Touch MBA in 2012, which has helped thousands of applicants get into the world's top MBA programs.

Darren hosts the ASE Podcast, which explores how self-employed creators, freelancers, and entrepreneurs are building their careers and managing their well-being. Darren graduated from Princeton University with a Bachelor's in Public Policy and International Affairs. He currently resides in Ho Chi Minh City, Vietnam.

Subscribe to Darren's podcast and writing at up-startist.tv/subscribe.

Notes

Introduction: Always Two Sides

1. *Less than I made during my first job 20 years ago:* In 2020 the average starting salary for Princeton University graduates was $71,300; the average starting salary for college graduates in the US was $52,500. Emma Kerr, "10 National Universities Where Grads Are Paid Well," US News and World Report, January 26, 2021. https://www.usnews.com/education/best-colleges/slideshows/10-national-universities-where-grads-make-highest-starting-salaries

2. *In 2019, 57 million Americans freelanced:* Edelman Intelligence, "Freelancing in America: 2019." https://www.upwork.com/i/freelancing-in-america/

3. *What I didn't expect was the cost:* I first saw the four entrepreneurial values of freedom, ingenuity, adventure and meaning in Dr. Sherry Walling's book, *The Entrepreneur's Guide to Keeping Your Sh*t Together: How to Run Your Business Without Letting it Run You* (2017). Dr. Walling is a licensed clinical psychologist and the founder of ZenFounder LLC, a mental health consultancy that serves entrepreneurs and high performing professionals. I highly recommend her book as a starting point for how entrepreneurs can safeguard their mental and emotional health.

4. *And instead of being happy about our choices:* Barry Schwartz explores how too much choice can paralyze in his book *The Paradox of Choice: Why More is Less* (Harper Collins, 2009).

5. *Starting a business is stressful:* Marcel Muenster, "There is a mental health crisis in entrepreneurship. Here's how to tackle it," World Economic Forum, March 22, 2019. https://www.weforum.org/agenda/2019/03/how-to-tackle-the-mental-health-crisis-in-entrepreneurship/

6. *the US had 26.5 million non-employer firms:* Federal Reserve Bank of New York, "Small Business Credit Survey: 2019 Report on Non-employer Firms," Fed Small Business. https://www.fedsmallbusiness.org/medialibrary/fedsmallbusiness/files/2019/sbcs-nonemployer-firms-report-19.pdf

7. *the share of adults who live alone has nearly doubled over the last 50 years:* Estaban Ortiz-Ospina, "The rise of living alone: how one-person households are becoming increasingly common around the world," Our World in Data, December 10, 2019. https://ourworldindata.org/living-alone

8. *85% of the jobs that will exist in 2030 haven't been invented yet:* Institute for the Future and Dell Technologies, "The Next Era of Human Machine Partnerships: Emerging Technologies Impact on Society & Work in 2030," 2017. https://www.delltechnologies.com/content/dam/delltechnologies/assets/perspectives/2030/pdf/SR1940_IFTFforDellTechnologies_Human-Machine_070517_readerhigh-res.pdf and McKinsey Global Institute, "The Future of Work in America: People and Places, Today and Tomorrow," July 11, 2019. https://www.mckinsey.com/featured-

insights/future-of-work/the-future-of-work-in-america-people-and-places-today-and-tomorrow

9. *"NBA Rookie Transition Program":* Pablo S. Torre, "How and Why Athletes Go Broke," Sports Illustrated, March 23, 2009. https://web.archive.org/web/20090811090257/http:/sportsillustrated.cnn.com/vault/article/magazine/MAG1153364/1/index.htm and AJ Neuharth-Keusch, "NBA Transition Program Helps Rookies Avoid Financial, Social Pitfalls," USA Today, August 15, 2017. https://www.usatoday.com/story/sports/nba/2017/08/15/nba-transition-program-helps-rookies-avoid-financial-social-pitfalls/565654001/

Practice 1: What's Your Shadow?

10. *Love means co-existing with and giving something space:* I learned this from Gay Hendricks' *Learning to Love Yourself* (2010). Dr. Hendricks earned his Ph.D. in counseling psychology from Stanford University and served as Professor of Counseling Psychology at the University of Colorado for over 20 years.

11. *I was setting myself up for failure:* To identify habitual and long-held patterns that hold you back I recommend Jerry Colonna's *Reboot: Leadership and the Art of Growing Up* (Harper Business, 2019)

12. *"The sign on our forehead":* Dan Andrews, Ian Schoen (Hosts) (January 7, 2021) The Price of Tomorrow (No. 579) [Audio podcast episode] In Tropical MBA Podcast. https://www.tropicalmba.com/jeff-booth/

13. *how can you respect and give healthy expression to your shadow:* To learn more about how your shadow can serve you, I recommend Deepak Chopra, Marianne Williamson and Debbie Ford's *The Shadow Effect: Illuminating the Hidden Power of Your True Self* (HarperOne, 2010).

Practice 2: Stuck? Seek Outsight

14. *"The outsight principle":* Herminia Ibarra, *Act Like a Leader, Think Like a Leader* (Harvard Business Review Press, 2015).

15. *"The more we mature, the more responsible our dreams become":* [The-Leap TV] (April 26, 2018) Kobe Bryant at USC PSI | Protect Your Dreams [Video]. Youtube. https://youtu.be/Ij4JNC7B94U

16. *Aerosmith's weekly "dare to suck" jam sessions:* Best-selling author Dan Brown shared the following anecdote about Aerosmith: "Strangely, I learned a lot about creativity from someone who is very different than I am. A man named Steven Tyler, who happens to be the lead singer of Aerosmith. I had the experience of sitting next to him and talking about the creative process. And he told me that Aerosmith has this ritual of once a week having a band meeting called Dare to Suck. Dare to suck, I thought? What could this possibly be? And Tyler said, 'Each one of us brings an idea that we think is probably terrible, and that we are embarrassed that we even have the idea. But we present it. And nine times out of ten, the idea is actually terrible. But one time out of ten you get Dude Looks Like a Lady or Love in an Elevator.'" https://www.masterclass.-com/classes/dan-brown-teaches-writing-thrillers

17. *the "real MVP":* In a heartfelt speech during his MVP award ceremony, NBA player Kevin Durant, called his mom the "real

MVP." [ESPN] (May 14, 2018) Kevin Durant delivers famous 'You the Real MVP' 2014 NBA MVP acceptance speech [Video]. Youtube. https://youtu.be/MN5YnVlDnIQ

18. *"This is the only life I have, so I want to make it meaningful":* Darren C. Joe (Host) (January 3, 2020) Making a Living by Making a Difference with Ho Thai Binh (No. 6) [Audio podcast episode] In ASE Podcast. https://upstartist.tv/ase/ho-thai-binh/

19. *"I love my family so much I would do anything for them":* Yous Sopanha talking to Katie Monk, "Life after Cambodia's Killing Fields," The Guardian, September 1, 2008. https://www.theguardian.com/world/2008/sep/01/cambodia-torture

20. *King, Warrior, Magician, Lover:* Robert Moore and Doug Gillette, *King, Warrior, Magician, Lover: Rediscovering the Archetypes of the Mature Masculine* (HarperOne, 1991).

21. *"I come as one, but I stand as ten thousand":* Oprah Winfrey talks about how being an African American woman has shaped her business career. [Stanford Graduate School of Business] (May 22, 2014) Oprah Winfrey: "I Stand As Ten Thousand [Video]. Youtube. https://youtu.be/0Li0J57d3YA

Practice 3: Can You Manage Yourself Better Than a Boss?

22. *asked thousands of people when they get their best ideas:* Michael J. Gelb, *How to Think Like Leonardo da Vinci: Seven Steps to Genius Every Day* (Dell, 2009).

23. *"digital shabbats"*: "Shabbat is a festive day when Jews exercise their freedom from the regular labors of everyday life. It offers an opportunity to contemplate the spiritual aspects of life and to spend time with family." Shabbat. (2020, October 16). In Wikipedia. https://en.wikipedia.org/wiki/Shabbat

24. *Being in a flow state:* Mihaly Csikszentmihalyi, *Flow: The Psychology of Optimal Experience* (Harper Perennial Modern Classics, 2008).

25. *control your physiology to compete at your highest level:* I first discovered performance rituals from Dr. James Loehr's *Mental Toughness Training for Sports: Achieving Athletic Excellence* (Plume, 1991) and then in his subsequent *The New Toughness Training for Sports: Mental Emotional Physical Conditioning from One of the World's Premier Sports Psychologists* (Plume, 1995). Dr. Loehr has also written about how "corporate athletes" can perform at their highest level in *The Power of Full Engagement: Managing Energy, Not Time, Is the Key to High Performance and Personal Renewal* (Free Press, 2003).

26. *Rest and recovery are necessary for our best performance:* Ferris Jabr, "Why Your Brain Needs More Downtime," Scientific American, October 15, 2013. https://www.scientificamerican.com/article/mental-downtime/

27. *Myers-Briggs Type Indicator (MBTI) personality inventory:* "MBTI Basics," The Myers & Briggs Foundation. https://www.myersbriggs.org/my-mbti-personality-type/mbti-basics/. You can take the MBTI online or find a certified MBTI practitioner at https://www.myersbriggs.org/my-mbti-personality-type/take-the-mbti-instrument/

28. *the authors knew me better than I knew myself:* Paul D. Tiger and Barbara Barron, *Do What You Are: Discover the Perfect Career for You Through the Secrets of Personality Type* (Little, Brown Spark, 2014).

Practice 4: To Have or To Be?

29. *Freelancers are more likely to feel they are living paycheck to paycheck than traditional employees:* Edelman Intelligence, "Freelancing in America: 2019." https://www.upwork.com/i/freelancing-in-america/

30. *To have or to be?:* I got this from Dr. Erich Fromm's *To Have or To Be?* (Open Road Media; Revised Edition, 2013), which was first published in 1976. Dr. Fromm was one of the twentieth century's leading social psychologist and philosophers.

31. *"The sage does not hoard":* Lao Tzu, Tao Te Ching, Chapter 81. Translated by Stefan Stenudd. https://www.taoistic.com/taoteching-laotzu/taoteching-81.htm

32. *money does increase subjective well-being:* Betsey Stevenson and Justin Wolfers have compared well-being across countries, across several different surveys, and found that there is no satiation point beyond which money doesn't increase subjective well-being. This strong relationship between income and subjective well-being holds for both rich and poor countries. Betsey Stevenson and Justin Wolfers, "Subjective Well-Being and Income: Is there any Evidence of Satiation," American Economic Review: Papers & Proceedings 2013. https://users.nber.org/~jwolfers/papers/Satiation(AER).pdf

33. *The average self-employed income in the US is around $48,000:* Elaine Pofeldt, "Nearly 30% of Americans are Self-Employed," Forbes, May 30 2020. https://www.forbes.com/sites/elainepofeldt/2020/05/30/survey-nearly-30-of-americans-are-self-employed/. There were 41,666 non-employer firms - those with no employees except the owners - that hit $1-2.49 million in revenue in 2018. Elaine Pofeldt, "Growth of Million-Dollar, One-Person Businesses Accelerates," Forbes, May 25, 2020. https://www.forbes.com/sites/elainepofeldt/2020/05/25/growth-of-million-dollar-one-person-businesses-accelerates/

34. *"Your business simply can't carry the weight of who you are":* Sherry Walling, *The Entrepreneur's Guide to Keeping Your Sh*t Together: How to Run Your Business Without Letting it Run You* (2017).

35. *"I must give up my desire to force, direct, strangle the world outside of me":* Shannon Lee (Host) (April 26, 2017) Be a Nobody (No. 43) [Audio podcast epi-sode] In Bruce Lee Podcast. https://brucelee.com/podcast-blog/2017/4/26/43-be-a-nobody

36. *Any time you hear blanket, absolute statements made in damning fashion, pay attention:* I highly recommend Mimi Kuo-Deemer's book, *Xiu Yang: The Ancient Chinese Art of Self-Cultivation for a Healthier, Happier and More Balanced Life* (Ixia Press, 2020) to learn about identifying your inner critic, and other ancient principles for self-cultivation. You can also listen to our podcast episode where we discuss this topic and her book. Darren C. Joe (Host) (March 19, 2020) Xiu Yang: The Ancient Art of Self-Cultivation with Mimi Kuo-Deemer (No. 15) [Audio podcast episode] In ASE Podcast. https://upstartist.tv/ase/mimi-kuo-deemer/

37. *"Everything around you that you call life was made up by people that were no smarter than you":* Interview with Steve Jobs by the Santa Clara Valley Historical Association in 1994. [Silicon Valley Historical Association] (October 7, 2011) Steve Jobs Secrets of Life [Video]. Youtube. https://youtu.be/kYfNvmF0Bqw

Practice 5: What's Your Perfect Day?

38. *Filling The Void:* Timothy Ferriss, *The 4-Hour Workweek: Escape 9-5, Live Anywhere, and Join the New Rich, Expanded and Updated* (Penguin Random House, 2009).

39. *President Barack Obama famously wore only two suits to avoid decision fatigue:* Michael Lewis, "Obama's Way," Vanity Fair, September 11, 2012. https://www.vanityfair.com/news/2012/10/michael-lewis-profile-barack-obama

40. *The following questions have helped me see my perfect day with more clarity:* Feel free to play my 10-minute guided audio available at https://upstartist.tv/perfectday/questions/

41. *Yet after 40 conversations:* The interviewees were 17-70 years old and hailed from 10 countries. About half were females. You can listen to the interviews at https://upstartist.tv/ase/perfect-day/

42. *humans have an innate psychological need to be autonomous, competent, and connected to one another:* You can learn more about self determination theory at https://selfdeterminationtheory.org

Practice 6: Who Are You Grooming?

43. *human beings could cognitively maintain roughly 150 casual friendships:* Robin Dunbar, "Neocortex Size as a Constraint on Group Size in Primates" Journal of Human Evolution, June 1992. https://www.sciencedirect.com/science/article/abs/pii/004724849290081

44. *Dunbar theorized that humans developed language to "groom" a larger number of tribe members:* Robin Dunbar, *Grooming, Gossip and the Evolution of Language* (Harvard University Press, 1998).

45. *"investing in a friend... is a much better source of security":* Thich Nhat Hanh, *Peace Is Every Step: The Path of Mindfulness in Everyday Life* (Bantam, 1992).

46. *The Cantril Self-Anchoring Striving Scale:* "Understanding How Gallup Uses the Cantril Scale," Gallup. https://news.gallup.com/poll/122453/understanding-gallup-uses-cantril-scale.aspx

47. *there is no satiation point beyond which money doesn't increase subjective well-being:* Betsey Stevenson and Justin Wolfers, "Subjective Well-Being and Income: Is there any Evidence of Satiation," American Economic Review: Papers & Proceedings 2013. https://users.nber.org/~jwolfers/papers/Satiation(AER).pdf

48. *higher incomes improve evaluation of life but not emotional well-being beyond an annual income of $75,000 USD:* Daniel Kahneman and Angus Deaton, "High Income Improves Evaluation of Life but not Emotional Well-being," Proceedings of the National Academy of Sciences of the United States of America, September 21, 2010. https://www.pnas.org/content/107/38/16489

49. *"Financial independence can lead to isolation"*: Sebastian Junger, *Tribe: On Homecoming and Belonging* (Twelve, 2016).

50. *individuals with adequate social relationships have a 50% greater likelihood of survival compared to those with poor or insufficient social relationships:* Julianne Holt-Lundstadt, Timothy B. Smith, and J. Bradley Layton, "Social relationships and Mortality Risk: A Meta-analytic Review," PLOS Medicine, July 27, 2010. https://journals.plos.org/plosmedicine/article?id=10.1371/journal.pmed.1000316

51. *Forming a second family, moai members meet regularly:* Aislinn Leonard, "Moai - This Tradition is Why Okinawan People Live Longer, Better," Blue Zones, August 2018. https://www.bluezones.com/2018/08/moai-this-tradition-is-why-okinawan-people-live-longer-better/

52. *"I wish I had stayed in touch with my friends"*: Bronnie Ware, "Top 5 Regrets of the Dying," The Guardian, February 1, 2012. https://www.theguardian.com/lifeandstyle/2012/feb/01/top-five-regrets-of-the-dying

Conclusion: Living the Questions

53. *"Be patient toward all that is unsolved in your heart"*: Rainer Maria Rilke, *Letters to a Young Poet* (W.W. Norton & Company; Revised Edition, 1993).

Made in the USA
Las Vegas, NV
13 May 2022